8/29/62

To Julius Livingston —

My very dear friend and mentor, & the conscience of Tulsa Jewry.

May his healing be swift and complete.

Rabbi N. L. Rosenthal

THE AMERICAN JEW
IN
SEARCH OF HIMSELF

OTHER BOOKS BY RICHARD C. HERTZ

The Education of the Jewish Child (1953)
Prescription for Heartache (1958)

BOOKLETS OF SERMONS

The Rabbi Yesterday and Today (1943)
This I Believe (1952)
Our Religion Above All (1953)
Inner Peace for You (1954)
Positive Judaism (1955)
Wings of the Morning (1956)
Impressions of Israel (1956)
Faith in Jewish Survival (1961)

PUBLICATION OF THIS BOOK

HAS BEEN MADE POSSIBLE BY THE TRUSTEES

OF

THE RICHARD COHN FOUNDATION

As A Memorial to the Memory of the Late

MAX SMITT

TIRELESS AND DEVOTED PRESIDENT

OF THE

Richard Cohn Foundation

THE AMERICAN JEW IN SEARCH OF HIMSELF

A PREFACE TO JEWISH COMMITMENT

by

RICHARD C. HERTZ, Ph.D.

BLOCH PUBLISHING COMPANY
NEW YORK

Library of Congress Catalogue Card Number 62-14460

PRINTED IN THE UNITED STATES OF AMERICA

To My Children

Nadine Hertz and Ruth Mann Hertz

and all their generation,

the pride and hope of

American Jewry

CONTENTS

INTRODUCTION

THE POST-WAR world introduced a whole new series of dilemmas for American Jews. Shaken to their souls by the holocaust of Hitler's scourge, confronted by the new Jewish state emerging out of historic necessity, faced with new adjustments in American living, the Jew in post-war America has turned both outward to his fellow Jews in the world over and inward to his inner self.

This book is written to help the modern American Jew understand why he has turned to his inner self. He knows he is a Jew, he wants to remain a Jew, but why and how and whither are questions of *Weltanschauung* that defy authoritarian solution. Not only must each generation search for new meaning and relevancy to the times, but each individual must think himself through and seek commitment to the abiding values of Judaism.

Commitment he needs, but to what end and through what means? The word commitment is usually considered in a theological context, but as the reader will discern, it has a sociological, situational frame of reference as well. Yet because the problems of Jewish commitment involve far more philosophical and existential implications than this book deals with, I have called it only a "Preface," not a conclusion nor even a guide. It is intended to crystallize the religious yearnings of the thoughtful American Jew seeking understanding of himself, his situation in America, his hopes for meaningful religious experience out of Judaism and Jewish identification.

As a Reform Rabbi and product of the Hebrew Union College-Jewish Institute of Religion, I have naturally written this from the point of view of Reform Judaism as I see it. That many Rabbis and laymen of Reform Judaism will see the problems in a different light or come up with different emphases is part of the Reform Jewish outlook: each must make his own judgment, each must come to his own seasoned conclusion. And I hope too that many outside Reform Judaism will find meat to chew on.

I am grateful to my own congregation, Temple Beth El of Detroit, where many of the ideas and opinions of this book were first expressed either in oral or written form, and particularly to those individuals who encouraged me to think that they should be expanded into book form.

I have had the encouragement and advice of several distinguished colleagues: Rabbi Samuel Silver, who thought there was room and need for such a book aimed at the modern Jewish adult; Rabbi Samuel Sandmel, whose advice and counsel were eagerly sought; Rabbi Robert I. Kahn, who was kind enough to make some detailed suggestions on the structure and sequence of this book; and Rabbi Dudley Weinberg, whose careful reading of the first draft and whose critical judgment did much to sharpen the text and separate the husk from the kernel. To each I owe the debt of friendship that stems from devotion to our common cause, the service of the God of our Fathers.

I am indebted to the trustees of the Richard Cohn Foundation, and especially to its president, Nate S. Shapero, for making this volume possible as a memorial to its late and esteemed president, Max Smitt.

My devoted secretary, Ruth Drazin, deserves a special

acknowledgment of gratitude for persevering the several drafts which she has been obliged to type.

For the forbearance and understanding of my wife during the happy summers when this book was written, I am particularly grateful.

R.C.H.

PART I

TOWARDS A RELIGIOUS PHILOSOPHY OF JUDAISM

1. *THE MARKS OF A RELIGIOUS PERSON*

THERE WAS a time when it was very simple for a rabbi to define a religious person. The answer of olden days was that a religious person is one who observed the *mitzvot* of Judaism, the *taryag mitzvot,* the 613 positive and negative commandments which Moses was reputed to have set down in the Torah and which were interpreted, defined, and clarified by the Talmud and the Shulchan Aruch. In traditional Judaism a religious man was the pious Jew, the Zaddik who sought the rule of *hesed* (lovingkindness) and searched for those values of salvation and grace that came from performing the will of God. His life was ruled by *kiddush hashem,* by a sanctification of God's name, and the holiness of life that invested all the minutiae of the Mitzvot.

Obviously, such a definition of a religious person seems "long ago and far away" from what a modern, Americanized Reform Jew accepts. If such were the only understanding of a religious Jew today, small wonder why many Jews say, "I'm not a religious Jew."

Reform Judaism arose a century and a half ago out of the need to square religious practice with modern circumstances of what the sociologists call "acculturation." Yet, neither time nor eternity can alter the basic marks of a religious Jew. The Bible and Talmud plus 3,000 years of glorious history have grafted certain distinctive marks onto the very heart of the eternal Jew. They cannot be erased nor eradicated save by excising the heart and destroying the life of the Jew.

What are these marks?

An Abiding Faith in God

First and foremost among the marks of a religious person, in our day or in any day, is *his awareness of a deep and abiding faith in God.* No man, be he philosopher or saint, has ever grasped the ultimate essence of God. Perhaps Moses came as close as any. The religious person sees the manifestations of Divine activity all about himself . . . in the dynamism of the universe . . . in the heavens and their starry constellations . . . in the laws of Nature and the unwavering, predictable regularity of the seasons . . . in the infinite varieties of earth, water, fire and air . . . in the rains and dew, the green and the growth . . . in all the vast panorama of existence. Such a universe is abundant evidence of some purposeful Intelligence constantly at work. Every creature in its own way, by its mere existence and by the precision of its functioning, offers daily testimony to the sources of Divine creation.

"The fool who hath said in his heart, 'There is no God,' "[1] sees in the world no sign of anything corresponding to the mind and spirit of purpose which exists in man, no sign of any universal spirit or reason with which we can hold communion; nothing but blind and unconscious force. He is an atheist.

The religious person, on the other hand, sees within

[1] Psalm 14:1.

him, above him, all about him, a universal and eternal reason or purpose with which he can correspond. He sees no conflict between religion and science. One is a faith, the other is a method. One depends on the disciplined mind, the other depends on the courageous heart. Both seek truth. Both deal with reality. Both are allies in the battle against ignorance, superstition and misery. He knows that religion begins with God. He may or may not be philosophic in bent of mind. It is helpful if he is, for philosophy gives intellectual support to faith, and its discipline of reason helps eliminate the superstitious and the fantastic from religion. Yet philosophy is no substitute for religion. Archbishop Temple once said, "The heart of religion is not the opinion about God wisely, such as philosophy might reach as the conclusion of its argument; it is a personal relation *with* God."

A religious person seeking that personal relationship with God finds its strongest fulfillment through prayer. Prayer is an attempt to identify one's heart and soul with God, to "link oneself with the inexhaustible motive power that spins the universe," to project oneself out of his own puny shell and latch on to the universal life-force which some call God and others leave nameless. Prayer focuses our thoughts and desires. It sorts them out and sums them up in our minds so that we see them in perspective, in relation to life as a whole. Prayer, thus, becomes not an attempt to wheedle favors out of God; nor an attempt to make God interrupt the predictable laws of Nature in order to make it rain or to stop the rain; nor can it be an attempt to persuade God to thrust Himself into the natural order of the universe and work a miracle for us to save someone from cancer. Prayer is rather an attempt to bring about an inner change within us.

Prayer does for us what a battery does for a flashlight. It provides current—power! Firmly connected to the juice of power, the flashlight shines brightly and lights up a dark pathway we are walking along at night. Well, prayer is like that. Without the communion with God that comes from prayer, life remains dark. But firmly connected with the sources of religious inspiration that comes with prayer, you find three dimensions opened up: *upward,* between yourself and God . . . *inward,* between yourself and some "still, small voice" we call conscience of soul . . . and *outward,* between yourself and your fellowman.

Or use another figure to describe something almost indescribable! God is like the great central broadcasting station of the universe. His transmitters send messages to us. Some of us have five-tube receiving sets, some seven or nine, some have twenty-one-tube sets. Static and interference prevent us from hearing completely. As we tune in, we hear lots of static until we're squarely on the right station. Prayer helps us get rid of the static; it produces better atmospheric conditions.

Without pushing the simile too far, you get the idea: all of us have a capacity to be in communion with the Supreme Being. Some have a greater capacity than others, and there are certain times in our lives when we are better able to commune with God. But that He exists and that man can draw strength and power from Him, inspiration for the daily task, courage for the problems of life—of that the religious person is sure!

Thus, a sense of commitment identifies the mark of a religious person. He senses the Psalmist's faith: "Into Thy hands I commit my spirit." He shares the blend of love and tenderness of the Psalmist's description: "As the hart panteth after the water brook, so panteth my soul after Thee, O God; my soul thirsteth for God, for the living God." [1]

[1] Psalms 42:2–3.

So! A religious person turns to God as a Sustainer and Helper! He feels the need for greater resources than his own. These he taps through prayer. He desires to give himself freely and generously to the purposes of God—to create and sustain those divine values worth his devotion. The result is a religious experience that makes him cooperate with others for good.

The faith of a mature, religious person is like a tree whose roots are deep in the stream of experience, whose trunk is sturdy enough to bear the brunt of the elements, a tree that brings forth its fruit in due season. Having weathered many storms, such faith is proved worthy and able to stand. Faith grows into faithfulness. Belief grows into trust. A person begins to understand why Job said, "Though He slay me, yet will I trust in Him." [1] Seasoned faith is the salt of life that loses neither its savor or flavor but purifies and preserves.

Difficult? Of course, it's difficult. Rare? Certainly it's rare. But others besides Moses succeeded. Never forget that Spinoza spent a lifetime searching for God, only to write in the closing sentence of his masterpiece, *The Ethics:* "All things excellent are as difficult as they are rare."

Religion, as G. K. Chesterton once commented wryly, has not been "tried and found wanting. It has been found difficult and not tried."

Gentle Relationships With Others

The second mark of a religious person is his *gentle relationship with other people.* The Jew has always believed that like the parson in Chaucer's *Canterbury Tales,*

[1] Job 13:15.

he must show the world not so much by his preaching as by his practice "a living sample of the truths he taught." The Talmud said 2,000 years ago: "Study is important in Judaism when it leads to action." [1] The ethics of loving one's neighbor as oneself, establishing society on the basis of justice and mercy and humanitarianism all indicate that *the marks of a religious person in Judaism have more to do with deed than creed, with action rather than diction.* The test of a man's religion is his character. Small wonder then, that the religion of Judaism has been so concerned with the character-building influences of life.

Kaufmann Kohler, who wrote the classic work on Jewish theology, saw in the advice of Hillel the best summary of the social ethics of Judaism: "If I am not for myself, who will be? But if I am only for myself, what am I? And if not now, when?" Duty to oneself and duty towards others are here placed side by side in inter-personal relationships.

The rabbis of the Talmud constantly decried envy and jealousy, pride and arrogance in men. Who is so repulsive today as the braggart who knows it all, the arrogant egotist who must dominate the center of attention? The rabbis of the Talmud counseled, "Humility is the greatest of all virtues." [2] The man who is puffed up with himself, full of wind and hot air, can scarcely be religious. Judaism teaches that arrogance is an evil trait not only because it hurts other people; it also hurts its possessor, for it sends him on a road that inevitably leads to frustration and unhappiness. The ambitious social climber, the scheming politician, the business man looking for influential contacts, the publicity seeker, the frustrated big-shot, the club woman hungry for recognition and status—all these well-

[1] Kidd. 40a.
[2] Ab Zorah 20b.

known types and a few others might remember the Talmud's warning: "Whoever runs after greatness, greatness will elude him; whoever flees from greatness, greatness will pursue him." [1] To which we can add: whoever runs after honors and recognition and publicity and influence, all these will elude him. Let the honor seek the man and not the man the honor!

The Golden Rule that Hillel offered—"What is hateful unto thee, do not do unto thy neighbor"—remains the core of Jewish ethics. Yet some people today are more interested in the Rule of Gold than the Golden Rule. They think everything and everyone has a price!

The Talmudic tract *Pirke Aboth,* read in the synagogue each year during the weeks immediately following Passover, has some wise injunctions to offer a person seeking to become a man of good will: "Let the honor of your friend be as dear to thee as thine own . . . Who is deserving of honor? He who honors others . . . If you have done your neighbor a little wrong, let it be in your eyes great; if you have done him much good, let it be in your eyes little; if he has done you a little good, let it be in your eyes great; if he has done you a great wrong, let it be in your eyes little." [2]

Judaism is concerned with building character. Building fine character uses the tools of ethics to shape personality. Humility, justice, lovingkindness, truthfulness, benevolence, decency, understanding—these are the classic virtues that mark the ethical outlook of the religious person. The person who enjoys gentle relationships with others must love mankind. He must feel like his brother's keeper—and act it. The Talmud asks with sharp insight: "Why did the Creator, God, form all life from a single

[1] Erubin 13b.
[2] Abot 1:6; Abot de Rabbi Nathan ch. 41.

ancestor? To teach the families of men not to lord one over the other with the claim of having sprung from superior stock, so that all men—saints and sinners alike—might recognize their common kinship in the collective human family." [1]

Being a man of good will often proclaims a religious person. The tragedy of history has been that we have had enough religion to hate one another but not enough to love one another. Cultivating what might be called "the inter-religious mind"—that is, one which does not think exclusively in terms of one's own "ism" or one's own doxology, but recognizes in others the right to their beliefs and acknowledges their contributions to civilization—this is the mark of the man of good will. He is not seeking tolerance, with its patronizing inference of condescending superiority, but appreciation and understanding. The inter-religious mind builds bridges across chasms of prejudice. The mark of a religious person is to be one of those builders.

Infinite are the examples one could cite from Judaism to illustrate the necessary traits of personality required for maintaining gentle relationships with other people. Judaism lumped them all together and called them *gemiluth hasodim,* "acts of lovingkindness," or to translate the same idea into the felicitous expression of the Good Will Movement, "cultivating better human relations."

Attachment to the Jewish People

Judaism does not believe that a religious person can live by himself in a vacuum, hermetically sealed from the

[1] Tosefta Sanhedrin 8:4.

give-and-take of interpersonal stimulus and response. The ideal person in Judaism is not the monk or ascetic who withdraws from life; but rather one who sallies forth into the stream of life and identifies himself with other like-minded people. *Attachment to the Jewish people* is therefore a third mark to note.

The need of belonging to the group is not only sound religion, it is sound psychology. To put your best foot forward and give your best, you must contribute yourself; you must identify yourself and share in the life of the community. You find a sense of life-enhancement and enrichment when you become part of something larger and more important than your own circle of values. All of us sense the need for greater resources than our own: "In unity there is strength" is a proverb that is just as true in Jewish communal affairs as in national politics.

In Judaism the focal point around which the Jewish community clusters has always been the synagogue. It has been the symbol of Jewish life, the source of its survival, the institution of its faith, the conservator of its heritage. Yet many choose to ignore it. Such a person says, "Why bother joining a temple? I can be religious without it. I can live the Ten Commandments and the Golden Rule in my home and in my business. I can think better alone than I can in a crowd. I can worship God in the hills or by the sea. Why go to services and listen to sermons when my religion is complete without the need of anything of that sort?" That sounds good, but does he? How often does he actually think of God on a mountain top, or pray when he is fishing? (I don't mean praying that he gets a bite!) The worship cliché has been worked to death. Grant that it is possible to worship God along the highway or in a football stadium! A Colgate professor once scored a hit when he said that a football should be gold-plated and placed on the chapel altar, since it has become higher education's chief object of worship.

Yet, the question of statistical probability arises. The chances are that God is worshipped more frequently in houses built in His name and set aside for His worship than any place else. One father said to his little girl, "Come on, we can say our prayers on the beach." To which the little girl replied, "But we won't, will we?" We can. But do we?

Rare is the person who can maintain his religious outlook without stimulus from those who share his values of devotion. None of us lives to himself. To say that we can be religious without belonging to a church or synagogue is arrogantly inaccurate. Anyone who sincerely tries to live a life of moral values in days like these needs all the assistance he can get. I know of no better place than the churches and temples of America to get that aid.

The parasitic hypocrisy of the unaffiliated is most clearly revealed when stripped of all pretense, he calls for the rabbi in time of joy or sorrow. Yet he ignores the institution which makes it possible for him to minister to the unaffiliated. He is a hitch-hiker. He depends upon others to carry the load.

To be unsynagogued means to cut oneself off from the heart that pumps blood into the arteries and veins of the Jewish people.

To be unsynagogued means to be disconnected from the spiritual currents that conduct energy and power into the life of the Jewish people.

To be unsynagogued means to be void of any meaning or reason for being a Jew. Why else should one continue to be a Jew save to be part of the great mother religion of mankind?

To be unsynagogued means to regard one's Jewishness as a burden of birth; to be saddled with a crushing handicap for life; to know only the liabilities of being a Jew without any of the assets; to know that it is tough to be a Jew and not to know how privileged it is to be a Jew.

To be unsynagogued means to be indifferent to the heritage and traditions which a hundred generations before us have preserved through three millennia of history.

To be unsynagogued means to ignore the spiritual source from which has come inspired faith, the dynamism, the mandate, to cope with problems of the poor and needy, the driven and dispossessed, the oppressed and the persecuted.

Not every one who is affiliated with a synagogue is a religious Jew; but certainly no one unsynagogued can expect to be a religious person. One cannot be a religious person without identifying himself in name and spirit with the synagogue of his choice. He can be a secular Jew, a checkbook Jew, a Kaddish Jew, a delicatessen Jew, a gastronomic Jew, a frightened Jew, a cardiac Jew, but never a religious Jew, and to my mind, never a real Jew.

A religious Jew is one who wants to stand up and be counted as such . . . who wants his family and his children to be part of the Jewish community . . . who feels no shame in saying, "Alone I am insignificant, but together with other Jews I am part of an eternal people!" Such a Jew feels a privilege in being able to add his strength and his enthusiasm to the joy of being a Jew. We need that spirit today badly.

Reverence of Spirit

The by-product, the carry-over from an abiding faith in God, gentle relationships with other people, and attachment to the Jewish people is a calm *reverence of spirit* that enables a person to ride out the storms of life with poise, and assurance, without fear or tension, a happier, better adjusted person. The word "reverence" is probably the key hallmark of a religious person.

Reverence for God! How badly our materialistic, dollar-crazy society needs reverence for God! When men forget God, they think they are omniscient. They know everything and no one can tell them anything. Pompous and power-hungry, they think they alone are responsible for their success. They seek to pyramid their power, as if to prove to themselves that they can play God. Napoleon Bonaparte tried that. William Randolph Hearst tried that. Adolf Hitler tried that. They all failed because when reverence for God vanishes, humility vanishes too, and worship of self is enthroned.

Reverence for Life! This component has been made vibrant by that great doctor of darkest Africa, Albert Schweitzer. It is his phrase, "reverence for life." Our times cry out for it. Nowadays the individual is losing his sense of significance. His soul is being fractured by schizophrenic tensions in society. The super-state is dwarfing individual freedom. Authoritarianism is taking over more and more areas of human welfare. At a time like this, reverence for life becomes the most precious thing in the world. After all, what is more precious than life itself? All our human efforts are bent toward preserving and enhancing its value. Medical science has prolonged human life. More people are living longer nowadays than at any time in history. Yet how are they living—standing on their feet or forced to their knees? And what are they doing with their extra years except to worry and fear and want? Reverence for life must teach our generation a few simple ideas about respect for personality and understanding of human dignity, human rights, human relations and human freedom.

Reverence for Truth is the third part of this little triangle of reverence. Without reverence for truth, life is nothing more than lies, cheats, hypocrisy, sham, pretense and counterfeit. Without reverence for truth, people are just phonies and fakes. Respect for self and respect for others comes only when we live the mandate of Moses: "Thou shalt love thy neighbor as thyself"—not more, not less.

What a different world of decency and morality if this idea of Reverence—for God, for life, for truth—were to seize the souls of men and regenerate them into members of the human race!

Visible Only When Applied

Religion, then, begins with the individual. Transformation of individual personality is crucial to the religious revival going on today. It is time to begin with ourselves. The personality of Moses, the hero of the Passover story in Judaism, with his abiding faith in God, his keen understanding of the need for gentle relationships with others, his devoted attachment to the people of the Covenant, his reverence for God, for life, for truth—all help us understand that even if we have fallen short, we can at least recognize the marks of a religious person and strive daily, in the humblest way, to develop these qualities in ourselves.

There is a well-known homily in the Talmud [1] that defines the marks of a religious person. Moses, it is told, set the number at 613, corresponding to the 613 positive and negative commandments that a faithful Jew must ob-

[1] Makkot 24a.

serve in his life. David came and reduced them to the eleven principles listed in Psalm 15. Isaiah came and reduced them to six: "He that walketh uprightly and speaketh righteously, he that despiseth the gain of oppression, that shaketh his hands from holding bribes, that stoppeth his ears from hearing of blood and shutteth his eyes from looking upon evil." [1] Micah came and reduced them to three: "It hath been told thee, O man, what the Lord thy God doth require of thee, to do justice, to love mercy and to walk humbly with thy God." [2] The Second Isaiah came and reduced them to two: "Thus saith the Lord: Keep ye justice and do righteousness." [3] Finally, the prophet Habakkuk came and reduced all the marks of a religious person to one: "The righteous shall live by his faith." [4]

The familiar Hasidic story of the soapmaker and the rabbi is pertinent. A soapmaker came to a rabbi and said, "I am here to inform you that I am through with Judaism. You have told us that the aim of religion is to bring peace, justice and charity into the world. But it has done nothing of the sort!" The rabbi invited him to take a little walk together with him in the park. There the two of them passed by a group of dirty-looking boys who were engrossed in play. "By observing those boys, you would conclude that soap is not effective," remarked the rabbi.

Nonsense," said the soapmaker. "Soap is never effective unless it is used."

"Ah, but the same is true of religion," countered the rabbi. "Religion, too, has value only when its principles are applied."

The marks of a religious person, like the effect of soap, are visible only when applied.

[1] Isaiah 33:15.
[2] Micah 6:8.
[3] Isaiah 56:1.
[4] Habakkuk 2:4

2. *WHAT IS BASIC IN BASIC JUDAISM?*

The tapestry of Judaism is beautifully woven together. You can see three colors blended together, three primary strands that give color and depth and strength to this tapestry. Don't try to distinguish these strands too carefully. You can't disentangle them altogether, for they are so tightly woven together in the warp and woof of time that no amount of picking can tear them asunder. Judaism is more than a stubborn knot. It is a living organism. It is a way of life.

Yet running through the strands is a common denominator of basic Judaism summed up so well by a classic statement in the Zohar: "God, Israel and the Torah are one." Here are three ideas, three concepts, three strands. How do these three form the cords that tie together the tapestry of basic Judaism?

The Existence of God

Judaism offers many arguments and proofs for the existence of God: *metaphysical arguments* from design, that the nature of Nature itself and the endowments of of man are unexplainable except through God . . . *arguments from causation,* that an existent universe is proof presumptive of a cause at least equal to itself . . . There are arguments *ethical,* the argument from man's emotional and moral needs, that without a God to give meaning to life and sanction to ideals, human existence is pointless, aspirations become frustrations and life devoid of purpose or hope . . . *Arguments from the experiences of men and nations,* that only the good is stable while evil tends to destroy itself, indicating an ethical power as the motivating force behind the universe . . . There are *arguments historical* based on the careers of peoples . . . and *arguments mystical* centering about the persistent reports, brought by some inspired souls in each generation, of inner illuminations resulting from direct contact with the Supreme Diety . . . And there are the *arguments of tradition* resting on revelation and prophecy recorded in Sacred Scripture.

Affirming God, Judaism permits wide latitude regarding man's conception of God; for after all, man is finite and mortal, incapable of reaching the full conception of an infinite and immortal Being. Still, Judaism says of God: He is One, not two, not three, not many. He is One, not none. Nothing that atheism or materialism offers can deter us from our conviction that God is the creator of all things: Spirit, Mind, Power, Reason, Purpose, Guide of History, Helper, Liberator, Savior, source of Salvation.

These are the God-concepts of basic Judaism with which men of all ages and temperaments have wrestled, even as have the sages and philosophers and mystics in every generation of history.

The Meaning of Torah

The second strand of thread in the tapestry of basic Judaism is the word *Torah.* Torah is an omnibus word. It has meant many things in different generations. It means a *book.* Five Books of Moses, 39 books of the Book of Books. It means *law,* 613 positive and negative laws. It means a *narrative* of our people's odyssey, a *history* of a great people, a *tradition* of stern morality. It means a *group of heroes*—Abraham, Isaac, Jacob, Joseph, Moses, and the immortal company that followed. It means a *people* wandering in the wilderness, a *covenant* at Mount Sinai to be faithful to the Ten Commandments. It means an *ethic* of justice and lovingkindness, of holiness and righteousness. Rabbi Jacob J. Weinstein thinks it means not only content but method as well, "a whole system of instruction and the climate of social opinion by which instruction in Torah was made the highest duty and first love of the Jew. It means the unique phenomenon of a people who made learning (Torah means that too) a popular, almost passionate concern of every Jew. Mothers were taught that the voice of children must always be heard studying Torah. Fathers were taught that if they did not bring up their children to study Torah, they would be denying these children their due heritage on this earth, and their own portion in the world to come."

This is the meaning of Torah, then, the precious heritage of our people which in every generation proved a *schoolhouse* for the unlettered, a *lighthouse* for the storm-tossed, a *blockhouse* for the besieged, a *book house* for the scholars, a *treasure house* for the people of the book. Torah has taught our people the value of self-knowledge, self-reverence, and self-control. It has exhorted our youth to carry on its proud tradition of learning, piety, ethics, decency. It has been the symbol of our faith, the source of our teachings, the banner of our people.

The Concept of Israel

The Jewish people—Israel—is the third thread in the tapestry of basic Judaism. Judaism is the *religion of the Jewish people.* That is a basic definition of our religious philosophy. A Jew is not a Jew in a vacuum. He is a part of the Jewish group. Professor Mordecai M. Kaplan wrote some years ago: "A Jew can no more be a Jew without belonging to the Jewish people than a soldier can be a soldier without belonging to an army. Merely donning the uniform and accoutrements of a soldier does not make him one, if he is not inducted into an army. And merely adopting certain characteristic habits and practices of a Jew does not make a man a Jew unless he feels his personal identification with the Jewish people in all ages and climes." [1]

The idea of Israel (not the State of Israel; that is something new, a present-day phenomenon that has reversed 2,000 years of Jewish life throughout the world), the *concept of Israel as a living people,* consists of "generations of individual men and women who feel bound together by memories of a common past, by a fraternal feeling and desire to be responsible for one another and to perpetuate the most sacred of their historic memories, and

[1] *The Reconstructionist,* July 2, 1954, p. 29.

by faith in the future significant role of the Jewish people in the life of mankind." [1]

Each individual Jew is identified as a member of the Jewish group. He looks to the group to give him faith, to help give meaning to his survival as a Jew, as well as courage and guidance for daily living. The group looks to the individual to give loyal support to those institutions and those ways of living on which the very life of the group depends.

What is basic in basic Judaism, therefore, is love of Israel, love of Torah, love of God. The three become one and the same, even as three tightly woven strands of threads become one and the same to form a beautiful tapestry.

The late Milton Steinberg concludes his brilliant book, *Basic Judaism,* by citing an exquisite and illuminating parable of the medieval Jewish philosopher Bahya ibn Pakuda. Once, we are told, a traveler was making his way through a difficult and perilous countryside when he came to the bank of a river too deep to be forded. Return he could not, nor remain where he was. How could he get to the other side? He bethought himself of the purse which dangled from his girdle, containing the gold pieces that were all his worldly wealth. In his extremity, he began to toss the coins one by one into the river hoping so to raise a pathway for himself over the river bed. In vain! The bag emptied, the river still could not be crossed. Finally, one gold piece remained. With this in his hand, he spied a ferry boat far down the river which in his frenzy he had failed to notice earlier. Regretting that he had wasted his treasure to no purpose, he hastened to the boat and felt fortunate that he had one coin left for the ferryman. Thus, he crossed to the other side and went his way.

Bahya ibn Pakuda had atonement in mind as its point.

[1] Mordecai Kaplan, *ibid.*

He was trying to say that penitence ought to be man's first expenditure but that it proves too often his last—the sole remaining device available to him when all else has been spent. With no violence to the parable, it can also be applied to the role of religion in life, and the relationship of Judaism to the Jewish people. For the wise and prudent, Judaism is the first coin in the purse—that disbursement of the spirit which makes possible the negotiating of life's most difficult passages, which enables men to go on their way safe and rejoicing. But for the foolish, the insensitive, the reckless, the undiscerning, it is the last coin in the purse, the one which—when every resource has been exhausted, when man is left with only his need and his desperation—then purchases a secure crossing to fresh possibilities and new hopes.

3. WHAT CAN MODERN JEWS BELIEVE ABOUT GOD?

Some time ago the *Ladies Home Journal* took a poll among its readers and concluded that 90 per cent of the American people believed in God. The poll did not reveal what the people believed about God. Indeed, it admitted that people don't know very much about God, except that they have a basic conviction that there is something in the Universe greater than themselves which has some degree of control or influence over their lives and with which they can and should have some kind of relationship.

Yet there are some modern sophisticates who say that God does not exist. They call themselves *atheists.* There are also some who say they don't know if God exists; they call themselves *agnostics.* There are many who say God does exist as the superhuman, supernatural creator, who is both transcendant and immanent in the universe. They are called *theists.* Then, there are those who believe in God as the creator of the world and judge of men, but they base their religious philosophy on reason alone. They are called *deists.*

I find it hard to follow the reasoning of the atheists. It seems like a very difficult thing to prove rationally and logically that there is no God in a universe which displays as much scientific and natural orderliness as the one in which we live. How can a scientifically trained person assert that nothing caused the cosmic order to come into being? Is it not a renunciation of reason to conclude that the universe just accidentally happened to spring forth into existence through no outer or higher cause?

There is a great lack of understanding among people between the extremes of theism and atheism, between agnosticism and deism. In fact, though people may glibly and sincerely say, "I believe in God," they cannot say very much more than that about the most basic affirmation of man's faith.

Indeed, the largest subject that any man has ever undertaken to define is concentrated in three words and nine letters, "What is God?" Edward Arlington Robinson answered the question rather neatly in his *King Jasper* when he said flatly, "I don't know what God is, but it's a name that answers us when we are made to think and feel how little we are responsible for what we are." Perhaps Robinson was thinking of Psalm 8: "When I behold Thy heavens, the work of Thy fingers, the moon and the stars which Thou hast established, what is man that Thou art mindful of him, and the son of man that Thou thinkest of him?"

Truly, we feel our inadequacy and humility in trying to answer the question of what modern Jews believe about God.

Where shall we turn? Judaism has recorded in the Bible a great spiritual adventure in the search for the meaning of God. Let us go back to the Prophets of ancient Israel.

The Prophetic Idea of God

It was the Hebrew Prophets of old who developed the Jewish idea of God, which despite the interval of three millennia has not faded nor diminished in validity. The Prophets taught the ancient people of Israel that God could not be worshipped except through righteousness and justice. Ethical monotheism lies at the heart of the prophetic concept of God.

The Prophet Amos censured his people for neglecting social righteousness even though they went through the motions of ritual rectitude. Amos taught the people that God did not command sacrifices nor vain oblations. God would not tolerate a religion which demanded that people observe the Sabbath or the new moon, and yet permitted them to exploit the economic necessities of the common people. Amos taught the people that God had only contempt for the mighty of the earth who would "sell the poor for silver and the needy for a pair of sandals," who would rob the widow and despoil the orphan. The mighty contribution of Amos, therefore, was this: justice is the irrevocable concomitant of religion and ethics the hallmark of the belief in One God.

From the Prophets, then, did the Jewish people learn that God demands respect for the humanity of the lowliest in the social order; that God despises the mighty and will depose them from power if their wealth is tainted or their success based upon the oppression of their fellow man.

Today, a modern Jew can still understand that God must be worshipped not so much by the words of our lips as the deeds of our hands. That is why we still return again and again to the prophetic teachings, so that we will understand that God is not some kind of police officer from Heaven who will give you a ticket if you don't do something, or if you do something that is forbidden. God is not an old man with long whiskers, who lives up on the sky. God is not a person that you can see. God is a spiritual force. You cannot see a spiritual force anymore than you can see the force of electricity or the force of gravity. But it is there. God doesn't have a human body and doesn't look like anything or anyone. That is anthropomorphism —the notion that God looks like and acts like mortal man. God is not an ethereal messenger boy whom we send for when we're in trouble or when we need something very badly.

Nor is God a cosmic bogeyman! Some parents use God for just that. If a child doesn't act right or disobeys, the parent says, "If you aren't good, God will be angry with you!" or "If you're bad, God will punish you!" Nothing could be more unfair to God, more disastrous to religion, nor more harmful to the child. Parents are often concerned about what they should teach their children about God. Of course, they should never teach their children anything about God which the child will later have to unlearn. In the final analysis, we communicate our beliefs about God to our children through what we practice rather than what we preach. You can't fool a child. He senses insincerity in an adult quicker than anyone you know. Anyone who thinks he is fooling a child is only fooling himself. The child learns his parents' true attitudes, inner convictions, by how they live, rather than by what they say. Professions of belief are borne out by one's way of living.

On Sunday mornings at Temple Beth El, I conduct a children's service for the very small primary children of our Religious School. I often talk to them about God, trying to help them understand the meaning of God. One of the hardest things for these little children to understand is that "God is never seen, and yet we know He's there, because we see the things He does and feel His loving care." I tell the children, "God is not a man, although we speak of Him as He. He is not at all like people and the things that we can see." One Sunday I gave them this little poem written by Dorothy Kripke which really suggests a great deal more than we realize about our understanding of God.

It isn't so important,
And it isn't even odd,
That we don't know so many things
About the ways of God.
The thing that matters most of all,
We're very certain of,
That God told people they must live
In brotherhood and love.

This poem, of course, gives us the essence of the prophetic interpretation of the meaning of God. God is best understood and worshipped through ethical action, through the ways of justice and righteousness that serve brotherhood and love.

"You Have to Trust God!"

To be sure, we gain an element of humility when we realize how limited is our own comprehension and understanding of the human quest for God. The mind of every philosopher from earliest times has been concerned with this problem, and there has been no answer—no real answer. The ultimate reason why man can never completely understand what is God is because we are human. As human beings we are born without consent or consultation. And as human beings we leave this earthly life without our consent.

Today we moderns are forced to believe. There are some questions that have no real answers. Maybe tomorrow will bring new lights. Maude Royden, the great British woman minister, said one time, "If I am asked to explain evil, I can't; if I am asked to explain why these things happen, I can't; but there is one thing I know. There is available a Power so that I can overcome every experience of life. Religion to me is not answering questions. Religion is not merely having an answer to all the enigmas and problems that you and I face. That isn't religion at all."

Religion is really being able to rise above those problems, to find the inner resources within one's self through communion with God, to face with courage and determination the issues of life.

For that we need to trust in God. We need Job's unshakable, abiding faith that come what may, "I shall not die but live and declare the glory of God."

And so spoke a modern child. "You have to trust God." Let Nellie M. Stewart tell her story about this child. "It was during the period of many earthquakes in Southern California. The papers were filled with reports of deaths and destruction. In a downtown San Bernardino building, on the fourth floor, this eleven-year-old girl was having a tooth filled. I was standing near. Suddenly, with that strange rolling motion common to earthquakes, the room began to sway. The hanging light above swung back and forth. But what to do? My daughter's tooth was in the process of being repaired. Her mouth was propped open, dental tools in her mouth. The quake lasted possibly four or five seconds—but when you are standing there, watching the results of it, those seconds drag out interminably. We couldn't run from the room with all its paraphernalia, and so we just waited. Soon all was still and the dentist continued. Leaving the building later I said to my daughter, 'Were you frightened?' She looked at me and grinned, 'Yes, I sure was,' she said, 'But I knew I couldn't get out of there right then. So I decided that sometimes you just have to trust God.' "

"Sometimes you just have to trust God" . . . How many times in our lives all of us face those situations, when there's nothing more we can do by ourselves, when we've reached the end of the road or the problem is too big for us, or the solution is beyond us. We just have to trust God. But it's easier and our confidence in the result is infinitely greater if we've learned to trust Him before some sudden emergency hits us.

It is easy to forget God in good times.

God and the doctor, all men adore
When sickness comes, but not before;
When health returns, alike requited,
God is forgotten and the doctor slighted!

These lines hang on the wall of a certain physician's office. Crisis religion doesn't go deep.

Why Seek God?

Why is it important that modern men should seek God in our time? It is important because a person is poor if he does not cultivate this side of his life, the spiritual life. A person is poorer if he lets his life go by without drawing close to God. Perhaps even more important, from the larger point of view, is that man stands in danger today of extinction. Because he has failed to draw closer to the spiritual foundations; because his inner life has deteriorated through disuse; because our sensitivities have coarsened through our materialistic preoccupations; because we have become more interested in sheer power and enthralled in manipulating physical things—we have pushed God aside and enthroned man.

Our civilization has grown huge and massive with our tanks and bulldozers and rockets and missiles. We have forgotten that once in another age, there were powerful giants of yesterday. The dinosaurs, who lorded it over the earth by virtue of sheer weight and power, became so big, so massive, that they lost the sensitivity necessary for survival. They ultimately became extinct and perished because of their sheer weight and size.

This must not become another dinosaur age. Somehow we have to recapture that life sensitivity if we are to keep ourselves from becoming so massive that we are concerned with power alone. We have to regain contact with the spiritual on-giving life force that we call God. Otherwise, our civilization, like the dinosaur age of prehistoric times, will become dissolved like the civilizations of Rome and Babylon and Tyre.

Searching for the meaning of God means seeking out those qualities of tenderness and grace, sympathy and understanding, charity, faith, hope and love. A thousand years from now, our descendants may look back upon twentieth-century man, upon his fumbling morality and his inadequate ethics, and think of us in much the same way that we today, with our jet planes and long-range intercontinental ballistic missiles, look upon the ox-cart transportation of the dark ages.

Maybe new worlds will be discovered not only in science, but also in religion. Who can tell whether what we call the Unknown today cannot become more knowable tomorrow? Who can predict whether some spiritual X-ray will not yet be discovered to throw light upon our God-quest, to give man at least a more complete answer to the question about the meaning of God than we now have?

One thing will be certain. We will need the creation of an augmented and more adequate spiritual vocabulary. Religion has not yet developed a sufficiently explicit lexicon to keep pace with the evolution of the God concept. When science enlarged its frontiers, it created new words to define new discoveries. Words like atoms and molecules and protons and electrons and isotopes are today elementary concepts in nuclear physics. But religion still employs the same terminologies used almost as far back as the Dinosaur Age. Our vocabulary has not kept pace with our ideas. We cannot find the word symbols to communicate the flashes of revelation nor describe the mystical moments of intuition. We call God in many names—Father, King, Providence, Shepherd, Holy One, Supreme Ruler, Sovereign of the Universe, and the like. We speak of God's Transcendence, Immanence, Omnipotence, Omnipresence, Omniscience; but neither these names nor these attributes seem to lift the searcher beyond the image that is essentially a product of the mind. We need not only more expansive ideas of God, but also new idioms and new speech-symbols to voice those ideas and to render them intelligible to man.

The Eternal Quest

Or is it impossible for finite man to comprehend the mystery of the Infinite Being? Is man destined never to see behind the cloak that separates the Holy One from the mortal gaze of man? Maybe the human mind is too hemmed in by its own limitations ever to approach the Ineffable Being of God.

Still, man never gives up the quest. Like scaling the heights of the Himalayan Mountains, man never ceases to attempt the impossible, no matter how many failures disappoint intrepid adventurers. Man still must keep trying to search for God . . . because he is man. This is the eternal quest . . . the quest for the Eternal.

Thousands of years ago, the Scripture chronicled the dramatic story of the man Job, torn by suffering, tried by sorrow. He searched his soul to find the meaning of God. One of Job's friends chided him:

> "Canst thou find out the deep things of God?
> Canst thou attain unto the purpose of the Almighty?
> It is high as heaven; what canst thou do?
> Deeper than the netherworld; what canst thou know? [1]

Perhaps it was with these lines in mind that a modern poet, aware that from Job's day to our own time no one has grasped the ultimate essence of God, penned this thought:

Go not, my soul in search of Him;
Thou wilt not find Him there—
Or in the depths of shadow dim,
Or heights of upper air.

For not in far-off realms of space
The Spirit hath its throne;
In every heart it findeth place
And waiteth to be known.

Thought answereth alone to thought
And soul with soul hath kind;
The outward God he findeth not,
Who finds not God within.

[1] Job 11:7–8.

And if the vision come to thee
Revealed by inward sign,
Earth will be full of Deity
And with His glory shine!

Thou shalt not want for company,
Nor pitch thy tent alone;
The Indwelling God will go with thee
And show thee of His own.

Then go not thou in search of Him,
But to thyself repair;
Wait thou within the silence dim
And thou shalt find Him there.

Frederic Lucian Hosmer

4. *HOW GROWN UP ARE YOU RELIGIOUSLY?*

A new phenomenon has struck many Reform Jewish Congregations in America. They call themselves "young marrieds." Not only are they developing future leadership for the congregation and the community, but they have provided a niche for young married couples who might otherwise have waited for years to find their way back to the Temple. These young married couples think. They are concerned with Judaism and Jewish life. They are not on the whole as critical as high school or college youth who sometimes want to bring down the walls, Samson-like, in youthful revolt against custom or tradition. Nor are they as smug or self-righteous as some older people who feel that everything ought to go on just as it has been, and that whatever has been done in the past should be conserved and perpetuated *status quo*. These fine Young Marrieds have the dynamic qualities of potential. As they bring their own children into the world, they sense a heavy responsibility of parenthood. They feel the need for maturity—social, emotional, psychological, religious maturity. For them life's purposes begin to lengthen. They are taking life seriously. They are asking each other questions about values. What satisfactions have real significance? What is really worth while? What does it all mean? How grown up is a person religiously? How mature is one's religious philosophy?

Three basic questions became criteria for this discussion, questions which must be answered personally.

1) Have you matured in your concept of God?

2) Have you reconciled any conflicts between religion and science?

3) Have you arrived at the decisive point where religion does something for your life?

These questions are by no means limited to young married people. They are pertinent for all Reform Jews, of whatever chronological age who have come of spiritual age and who need to test their religious maturity.

Your Concept of God

Do you still think of God in anthropomorphic terms? Do you still think of God as a great big superman who punishes you when you're evil and rewards you when you are good? Does God to you mean an old man on a throne somewhere up in the sky—a Santa Claus idea?

Because so many thoughtful people have rejected this child-like concept of God, they think they are atheists. Nothing could be farther from the truth. It is normal and natural for little children to have a "father image" of God in this way; but just as children outgrow childish ideas about other things, so they outgrow naive notions about God. The tragedy comes when instead of maturing in their ideas of God, as they do in other values, they reject what they remember from childhood and replace it with a vacuum of nothingness. Many people thus regard themselves as atheists simply because they don't believe there is an old man Santa Claus up there in heaven. In so doing, they condemn themselves to spiritual immaturity and to stunted, unsatisfying religious convictions.

A mature understanding of God has something to do with recognizing that a Divine Intelligence created the universe . . . that law and order govern the affairs of Nature . . . infinite . . . incomprehensible . . . inscrutable . . . above and beyond the ken of mortal man. A mature religious person understands it is utterly impossible for any human being to know everything about God.

The sages of Judaism tell about an ancient scholar who thought he knew all about God. The teacher decided to give a public lecture in which he would tell people everything there was to know about God. While preparing himself for his lecture, he happened to walk along the seashore where he saw a child digging in the sand. He was puzzled by the fact that the child was carrying water from the ocean in a spoon and putting it in a hole he had dug in the sand. The scholar asked him what he was doing. The child replied, "I'm going to take all the water out of the ocean and put it in this hole."

"But that is impossible," exclaimed the scholar. "You can't ever empty the ocean of water. It is boundless, endless."

Then he thought to himself, "Am I not as foolish as the child? How can I, with my small brain, hope to grasp the infinite nature of God?" Only then did he realize how impossible it was for any human being to know everything about God.

God doesn't change, but people's ideas about God change. The earth didn't change one bit when people stopped supposing it was flat and began to understand it was round. It was always round, even though centuries and centuries ago some people thought it was flat. In like manner, God has always been the same. It is our ideas of God that have changed.

When you were a little child, your notions about most things were quite different from what they are now. Once you may have felt that the music coming from your radio was actually being played inside the little box; or that there were real people behind the motion-picture screen in the theater actually speaking the parts. As you grew older and acquired a more adult, more mature understanding of these things, you came to know something different.

Exactly the same process goes on concerning your idea of God. At one time it was quite natural and normal to have thought of God in a father image as a dignified old man with whiskers sitting on a throne somewhere up in heaven. We may not be sure of what God is like as mature grown-up people; but we should not be surprised that our ideas are different from those of our ancestors, or even from those we held ourselves when we were little children.

What do mature people mean when they talk of that remarkable three-letter word—God? They visualize God as the force or power we recognize throughout the world of nature, the force which is responsible for the amazing order, harmony, purpose, design, plan which we discover everywhere from the remotest star in the heavenly bodies to our own physical bodies. None of this remarkable universe, our mature minds tell us, could be mere accident or coincidence, any more than, as the medieval Hebrew philosopher Bahya ibn Pakuda once told us, a bottle of ink accidentally spilled could possibly form itself into the characters and letters, the words and laws of the Book of Books, the Bible. Some supreme intelligence, some master mind, must have known how to use that ink, how to fashion its indelible coloring, into the divinely inspired book that mankind has come to revere.

Another mature point of view considers God to mean the master ideal, the ethical goal, the pattern of perfection toward which we are evolving and for which we ought to strive throughout our lives. God becomes the sum total of all our ethical ideals, each magnified to perfection, all joined together as a great common goal leading to salvation.

Or we can say that God is the superhuman force or power which has been patiently working its way upward through the long course of evolution, helping life forms to develop from the simplest, invisible protozoa to the mind, the conscience, the creative genius of man. The Psalmist sang those words long ago:

> O Lord our God,
> How glorious is Thy name in all the earth!
> When I behold Thy heavens, the work of Thy fingers,
> The moon and the stars whichThou hast established,
> What is man, that Thou art mindful of him?
> Yet Thou hast made him but little lower than the angels,
> And hast crowned him with glory and honor.
> Thou hast made him to have dominon over the works of Thy hands;
> Thou has put all things under his feet . . .
> O Lord our God,
> How glorious is Thy name in all the earth! [1]

Or we can interpret God in a more personal way to mean the power or force within ourselves which strengthens and sustains us in our efforts to reach the goal of perfection . . . which makes it possible for us to progress toward that goal if we cooperate? Part of this power within us we call conscience, the still, small voice that is never silent.

These are not, as Rabbi Roland B. Gittlesohn reminds us, four different or mutually contradictory concepts of God. They are part of the same idea, though dif-

[1] Psalm 8.

ferent aspects of it. It is like approaching a great mountain. It appears different from different directions and different perspectives. Sometimes it is difficult to believe you are looking at the same mountain when you view it from a new angle.

What we are doing then, so to speak, is to walk around the idea of God . . . look at it from different angles and perspectives. Theodore Herzl once referred to the word God as "this beloved, old, wonderful abbreviation." For us also, the word God can be a wonderful abbreviation or symbol of all that is inscrutable, unknowable, awesome, infinite, transcendent, immanent . . . or to use less theological terms, the symbol of the best, the symbol of the order, law and purpose that exist throughout the universe.

No, the world of reality did not just 'happen.'

The universe, physical and moral, is a cosmos not an anarchy. It is "the manifestation of a creating, sustaining, animating, design-lending spirit, a mind-will, or to use the oldest, most familiar and best word, a God."

Science and Religion

How else can thoughtful people test their religious maturity? Not so long ago, people were saying that science is incompatible with religion. Young people who were taught the Genesis story of creation became completely non-plussed when in high school or college they discovered science, when Darwin's theory of evolution was explained sensibly and rationally, when the scientific method of observation, classification and deduction was embraced intellectually. Young people in college found it difficult to resist the temptation thus to identify science with facts, religion with fables. They didn't understand that science never created a fact nor destroyed a fact. Science merely describes what *is*. Religion's task is to describe what *ought to be*.

People overawed by the wonders of science sometimes forget that science has brought out new facts just as religion has brought out new ideas. To change is the very life of the universe. Life means change. Whatever or whoever has stopped growing is dead. For example, science has completely changed and abandoned the Ptolemaic system of astronomy. Today's evolutionary theory has persuaded scientifically trained minds that God created the world not like a carpenter making a chair but more akin to the way a flower grows, germinating from a seed, gradually unfolding and developing. Science has demonstrated that the world was not created exactly 5,721 years ago on last Rosh Hashana, but has come about through billions of years of growth and development, through the stages of mineral life, plant life, lower animal life, higher more complex life and finally man.

The problem of miracles also disturbs people seeking religious maturity. On the one hand, the Bible's tradition accepts as historical truth the miracles mentioned in the Biblical narrative—the dividing of the waters of the Red Sea, the guidance of the Israelites by a moving pillar of cloud by day and fire by night, the feeding them in the wilderness with manna that fell in a double portion on the sixth day of the week but did not fall at all on the Sabbath, or even the halting of the sun in its path for Joshua. How could such miracles have happened?

In our day, when man has achieved such marvels of control over nature, when he has conquered space and time by a technology that relies upon the regularity of natural law, absolute belief in such miracles undermines mature religious faith. People say, "If this is religion, I won't buy it!"

What they fail to understand is that the natural laws of the universe are much more wonderful than the so-called miracles. Centuries ago our ancestors were simple folk as far as science was concerned. Ancient man knew much less about science than we do today; but he was no less curious. And what he failed to understand he simply called "a miracle." If it suddenly rained after a long drought, it was a miracle! If the sun disappeared in what today we call an eclipse, it was a miracle! If huge torrential winds appeared off-land to blow back the Red Sea waters and provide an escape from the jaws of certain death, it was a miracle! If the secretions of certain tamarisk trees and bushes of the desert condensed at night-time to form crystals or beads of sweet, sticky substance edible and nourishing, it was manna from heaven—a miracle! Scripture relates as miracles what scientists and archaeologists today understand as ordinary, normal, natural operation of the world of 3,000 years ago.

Religion is not in conflict with science nor science with religion. But religion is not a substitute for science, nor is science a substitute for religion. In our time, Albert Einstein wrote in his autobiography, *Out of My Later Years,* "Science without religion is lame. Religion without science is blind." If each tends to its own business and does not poach on the other's territory, religion and science can and should live together and benefit from each other. Einstein symbolized that point of view. For him, a religious person was one who liberated himself from selfish desires, who found meaning to life, who dealt with values rather than materialistic things, who felt there was a goal to human existence and who could rise above hatred because he knew that love unites while hate destroys.

Robert A. Millikan, a Nobel Prize winner in science,

published his autobiography about the same time that Einstein's *Out of My Later Years* came out. Millikan insisted that human progress rested upon two supreme elements, the spirit of religion and the spirit of science. Without either the world cannot go forward. To him the essence of religion is to develop the immediate impulses, appetites, and desires to the larger good of mankind. He believes with all his heart that the combination of science and religion provides the sole basis for rational intelligent living. He finds God in nature and in human nature, and believes that the interplay between the two can lift man to heights sublime.

I find no conflict between science and religion. Science teaches what is. Religion teaches what ought to be. Science describes. Religion prescribes. Science analyzes what we can see. Religion deals with what is unseen. Each can help the other.

What Does Religion Do For Your Life?

This question brings us to the heart of religion in action: what does it do for your life? What difference does it make in your values and goals? Is Judaism made up entirely of holidays, festivals, rites, ceremonies, customs and practices, and when you observe them piously, are you then satisfied that you have done all that the Lord requires of thee? Or do you still hear the still small voice of Micah adding his prescription: "Do justice, love mercy and walk humbly with thy God"?

Professor Henry Nelson Wieman, formerly of the University of Chicago, pointed out that religion becomes vital in the maturing processes because it awakens interest in other persons by accenting unselfish attitudes. It provides common interest and mutual purposes to draw people together and thus overcome lonely isolation in significant social companionship. It requires a sharing of values for the welfare of others. It furnishes standards and patterns of socially acceptable behavior. It encourages service on behalf of the needs of others. It stimulates communication of ideas as well as creative thinking. It impels constant adjustment and growth through diversity and continuous chance. It facilitates cooperation, mutual aid and effective social organizations. It brings the social heritage to the individual and puts him in touch with significant achievements and values of the group. It gives social and moral support to the member in a way that fortifies him with a sense of security and personal worth.

There are three dimensions of religion: *Upward,* between man and God; *inward,* between man and himself; and *outward,* between man and man. Each is fundamental to the religious genius, yet if we can speak of one as more important than the others, Judaism would teach that it is the third—the building of society upon religious principles. This is the crucial test of the values of religion in the lives of men. Unless this is the area emphasized by organized religion, then activity in the first two dimensions is sterile and barren. The search for God is fruitless and the quest for self-adjustment is impossible. Only as religion is a vital force in the battle for progress, peace and justice, does the religionist prove that he is sincere in his approach to God and realistic in his desire to fulfill himself. Religion—complete religion—is more than prayer and self-improvement. These must lead to dynamic social action. It was just this that was in the mind of the prophet Amos when he denounced his contemporaries who were apparently punctilious in formal observance but who failed to follow the essential third dimension of religion:

> "I hate, I despise your feasts,
> And I will take no delight in your solemn assemblies.
> Yea, though you offer Me burnt offerings and meal offerings, I will not accept them . . .
> Take thou away from Me the noise of thy songs.
> Let me not hear the melody of thy psalteries,
> But let justice flow like water and righteousness as a mighty stream."

Religion, especially the ethical mandates of prophetic religion, is not an escape from the world nor an "opiate for the masses" in place of social reconstruction. It is rather the dynamic force that challenges man to protest against injustice and exploitation. The ancient prophets of Israel taught us how their ethical mandates can become a leavening force in the souls of man, giving him lifting power, helping him out of the depths of degradation and enabling him to climb toward the heights of spiritual triumph.

Social justice, the quest for truth, the battle for human dignity, the cultivation of public conscience, the struggle against exploitation—these are just a few of the dynamic values of mature religion. This is a Judaism which preaches not pessimism nor fatalism, but challenge and response. This kind of prophetic religion rejects every move to rob men of the opportunity to improve their lot and change things for the better. The prophetic heritage of mature Judaism makes it a religious obligation to throw oneself into the battle for human rights, for human dignity, for human betterment.

To be sure, there have been times in the past when men have faced tough problems and diabolic evil. They did not master all the difficulties, but they did master themselves. And that is something for mature people to learn. They learned to adjust themselves to the conditions of life. They made conditions the best possible and then made the best of conditions. They discovered hope from mature religion . . . hope to overcome frustration, hope to translate prophetic ideals into practical reality, hope to harness the drive of the universe into one's own inner soul, hope to find one's place in the world through service to mankind.

The search for religious maturity is itself a quest that helps one to grow up spiritually. Like searching for happiness, the reward is not in the final goal but in the quest itself.

Religious Maturity

What, then, can a mature religion do to your life? It can supplant fear, worry, and wearing haste with calm self-possession. By viewing things, as Spinoza counseled us, *sub specie aeternitatis,* "under the aspect of eternity," religion can focus our perspectives so that great things look great and small things look small. By breaking down the barriers between man and his fellow man, it can involve us in building bridges of better human relations so that brotherhood can become a two-way highway. By uniting us in fellowship with other worshipers, it can break down our sense of isolation in "the lonely crowd" and unite us with those who sincerely seek to build, "to perfect the world under the Sovereignty of God."

The man with a mature religious philosophy knows that it is not enough to have an intellectually respectable concept of God. As important as it is, it is not enough to reconcile science with religion and square one with the other, knowing that each has its sphere. What is vitally important is for man to understand that religion must do something to his life. It must change his outlook from parochial isolation to humanitarian universalism. It must lift his viewpoint from himself alone and identify his creative efforts with society, with his neighbor who must become his brother. Religion must translate itself into action, for religion is not just a way of looking at certain things but a certain way of looking at all things. Religion is not just believing but doing . . . acting . . . living because of what you believe.

5. *THE QUEST FOR AUTHENTIC RELIGION IN MODERN JUDAISM*

Three Generations in America

The immigrant story of how people came to America and adapted themselves to the new world has become part of the American heritage. The rebellion of the second generation against the foreign ways of their parents is also part of that story. In the case of Jewish immigration, the religion of orthodox, traditional Judaism was often associated with the foreignness of the immigrant Jews. Indeed, in many ways the only Judaism the second generation knew was the foreign immigrant culture associated with their parents' Jewishness. Rejection of foreignness often meant rejection of Judaism and Jewishness, for the second-generation Jews in America were desperately anxious to become American, "one hundred per cent so." They were resentful of the immigrant culture which the older generation seemed so eager to transmit to them.

The second generation of American Jews, therefore, often became a weak link in the chain of Jewish continuity. Some of the second generation were attracted to secularism. Some became radicals and internationalists. Some became Socialists or Communists. Some became Zionists. And some tried to stray as far as they could from any religious identification.

The emergence of the third generation of American Jews, however, took a different tack. Among other immigrant groups, the emergence of the third generation usually meant the approaching dissolution of the ethnic group. For example, all that the third generation of the Italian or the Polish group in America could remember was the religion of the grandfather. The immigrant language and culture and the way of life were irretrievably gone. So the emergence of the third generation usually meant the disappearance of the "Italianness" or the "Polishness" of the group.

With the Jews, however, it was different. First and second generations of Jews in America repeated the familiar immigrant pattern. Immigrant foreignness meant but an anxious effort to overcome that foreignness and become "American." But the third generation of American Jews, instead of somehow getting rid of their Jewishness as the Italians were getting rid of their Italianness and the Poles of their Polishness, actually began to reassert their Jewish identification and return to their Jewishness. They, too, were striving to remember what their parents had so often striven to forget, though the content and consequences of their remembering were strikingly different. Hansen's law of social history has operated among American Jews in their third generation's interest. "What the son wishes to forget, the grandson wishes to remember."

Recently an illuminating survey was made of an Eastern seaboard city of 127,000, with a Jewish community of some 8,500. It was found that among those who were interviewed, both young and old, the overwhelming number wished to retain their Jewish identity. This desire was so strong as to constitute a firm obstacle to either assimilation or to inter-marriage.[1] The survey also found that fully 97 per cent of the adolescents, teenagers from 13 to 20, all of the third generation, when asked what is a Jew, replied in terms of religion.

This reply suggests an interesting conclusion.

Jewish Suburbia

When the younger, native-born third generation which is thoroughly acculturated into American life identifies itself in religious terms, one can understand the phenomenal growth of synagogue affiliation that has taken place since World War II. This is particularly the case in suburban areas in and around the major metropolitan cities of America, like New York, Chicago, Philadelphia, Boston and the like. Young married, third-generation American Jews moving into these suburban areas report that their identification registers on a religious basis. In Brooklyn or the Bronx or the west side of Chicago, they didn't have to prove their Jewishness. They lived in a self-contained ghetto. Their neighbors, their friends, their children's playmates were all Jewish. But in Suburbia they found Christian neighbors. They needed to escape from the sense of not being wanted by Christians, and the synagogue—not the Jewish Center and not a Jewish Club and not a Jewish Lodge and not a Jewish Welfare Federation—but the synagogue, the temple, became the answer to their anonymity and alienation. Such Jews may often have been utterly estranged from the traditional values of Judaism which for them had an association with the immigrant foreignness of

[1] Marshall Sklare, *Form and Expressions of Jewish Identification,* unpublished report presented at the Tercentenary Conference of American Jewish Sociology, Nov. 27–28, 1954.

their parents; but when it came to raising their children in a non-Jewish atmosphere, to striking roots in a suburban, non-Jewish community, they found themselves unable to endure the yoke of non-conformity. They wanted a Sunday School. They wanted their children to go to a Temple on Sunday morning the way their playmates went to a church. They themselves wanted Jewish company and Jewish friends "after five o'clock." Where else but the Temple? In suburban America today, the fashionable pattern of middle class status has involved belonging to some church or synagogue. Jews are no different. They don't want to be different. They are part of what David Reisman calls "the lonely crowd."

As Albert I. Gordon's research on this subject has shown, it is the religious pattern that has emerged in the suburban communities; and as the suburban Jewish community becomes an increasing element in American Jewry, the synagogue will come to symbolize the institution that represents the suburban Jews.

In an article in *Commentary* about "The New Suburbanites of the 50's," [1] Harry Gersch suggested one reason for this phenomenon: "In the cities . . . we found it unnecessary to think seriously of ourselves as Jews." In the city, living in a Jewish neighborhood, one may unconsciously continue to accept one's Jewishness in terms of ethnic belonging, but in the suburbs, as in many small towns, this is no longer possible. One must begin to think seriously of his Jewishness, and the only possible outcome of such thinking in present-day America is identification with the Jewish religious community, which means affiliating with a synagogue or temple of one's choice.[2]

The suburbia problem is not limited to Jews. Recently I attended a luncheon meeting of the United Com-

[1] *Commentary,* March, 1954.

[2] Will Herberg, *Protestant, Catholic, Jew,* page 220, footnote 45.

munity Services in Detroit. One speaker told of a family moving to the suburbs. On the night before the moving van was to arrive, the child said in his bedtime prayers: "Goodbye, God! We're moving to Bloomfield Hills!"

Religious Identification

Thus, as the third generation of American Jewry comes of age in the second half of the twentieth century, it seems quite apparent that the religious institution and the religious community of the American Jew will move to the forefront. Other ideologies which made their appeal to Socialists, Bundists, Yiddishists, or Zionist organizations, are in the decline. It is the religious organizations of American Jewry, the synagogues and temples of the Reform and Conservative groups primarily, which are moving forward both in numbers and in influence. This is true in many sections of America. Forces of Americanization and acculturation are responsible in large measure for this social development because it is the trend of the times. The pattern of America includes a common core of religious Americanism, for the American way of life holds out values of individual freedom, personal independence, human dignity, community responsibility, social and political democracy, sincerity, restraint in outward conduct, and many other values embodied in the American way of life. Religious association has become the primary frame of reference, the context of social identity for the third generation of American Jews.

To illustrate the extraordinary pervasiveness of religious identification among present-day Americans, recall how the militant secularist, the atheist, the freethinker, so familiar in the nineteenth century, are now vanishing figures. Practically all major types of American religion have staged a comeback. "Religion has become a fad," said the late Canon Bernard Iddings Bell of the University of Chicago. Church membership is at an all-time high with about 60 per cent of the American people being officially affiliated as members of churches and temples; whereas at the opening of the nineteenth century not much more than 10 per cent or 15 per cent of the population were affiiliated. Fifty years ago church membership stood at something like 36 per cent of the population, and even in 1926, it was only 45 per cent. Along with other figures on membership, attendance, Sunday School enrollment, expansion in church construction, organization of new churches and congregations, all-time high in giving, it is a far cry from the 1920's when religion and the churches were in retreat, when faith was taken as "a sign of intellectual backwardness or imbecility, and the initiative had passed to the emancipated debunkers of the superstitions of the Babbitts and the Bible Belt."

There has likewise been a renewal of religious interest in intellectual areas, in the books that have been written and in the best sellers that reach the top of the "hit-parade." Colleges and universities are creating Departments of Religion which previously did not exist. There is a genuine stirring on the campuses of the nation. Today the *avant-garde* is becoming old-fashioned. Religion is now the latest thing.

Added to the sociological factors are the psychological factors where the contemporary crisis of western civilization has brought such a sense of insecurity to men everywhere. The hydrogen bomb, two world wars in one generation, the appeal of religion as the best hope of peace in the world today, seem to explain in some measure why our younger people need spiritual security and are turning to those enduring institutions of mankind which symbolize permanence and stability in a world falling into chaos.

Even the atomic scientists at Oak Ridge, Tennessee, who had shown little interest in the political status of their new community, have shown an intense concern for building their religious institutions. One Oak Ridge atomic scientist was asked what he did when he was through with his scientific labors in the laboratories, and he replied, not without significance, "After we are through working on the atomic projects, we pray."

Now that man can no longer look for salvation to science, to progress, to economics, or to politics, our age is turning to religion, to faith, for a viable philosophy of existence in the spiritual chaos of our time.

A Religion of Convenience?

In the light of all this—the return to religion, the revival of interest in religious matters, the search for a viable philosophy of existence, the reclaiming by the third generation of what the second generation has discarded—one may properly ask, "Is American liberal Judaism just a religion of convenience? Is it a lazy man's approach to Judaism? Or is there something authentic in the religious experience of modern Judaism?"

Many people feel that the religiousness characteristic of America today is very often a religiousness without religion, with almost no content. All too often it seems more like a way of sociability or belonging than a way of reorienting life to God. It lacks serious commitment, serious inner conviction.

How about this problem? Is there anything authentic in modern Judaism—or is it simply a religion of convenience? Let's approach the question this way. Everyone knows that today one of man's primary needs is to feel secure. We hear a lot of talk about security nowadays—family security, emotional security, social security, economic security, national security, collective security. Our whole generation is seeking security today against the insecurities of poverty, sickness, unemployment, old age, war. And yet we need to be on guard against falling into the trap of mistaking comfort for civilization. Material ease is not necessarily culture, even though we see so much in advertising today about making things easier—easier washing, easier cooking, easier driving, easier traveling, easier living. Security is not always a matter of ease or comfort. Strength of character, perseverance, self-reliance, do not always come to the person who has had things made easy for him.

The same is true about religion. A religion of convenience can be a danger. Some people turn to religion for what it can do for them. They want it to bring escape from worry, fatigue, sleeplessness and sorrow. Such people are more anxious to learn how to relax than how to stand up to life. That word "relax" has become the magic formula of our time. It is almost a national cult. But life isn't always relaxing. Some people like to jog along the old, well-worn ruts and be left undisturbed. They remind one of the sign that often hangs outside the door of a hotel room when a man wants to sleep the next morning. He puts out the sign, "Do Not Disturb." This is the kind of sign many people hang outside their doorways of life. "Don't disturb me! Don't bother me! I don't want to be upset! I want to relax!"

Fortunately, liberal religion *is* the kind of religion

that bothers a person. It is *not* a religion of convenience.

What are the alternatives? Orthodox religion offers a person the convenience of not having to change at all. Everything is prescribed by rabbinic law. The individual has only to follow the *halacha.* Orthodoxy demands no necessary adjustments to anything new or different. It carries no bothersome nuisance of having to square oneself with sociological change or with scientific progress. Although orthodox Judaism offers an enormous reservoir of spiritual wisdom and moral strength, it does not have to be concerned with adjusting religious practices to aesthetic standards. Being in harmony with the needs of the times is neither necessary nor desirable. It is a kind of *table d'hôte* religion—everything is served with it. Nothing comes a la carte that you can take or leave.

The other alternative to liberal religion is paganism. The pagan has the convenience of no obligations at all. To the pagan there are no services to attend, no congregational projects to support, no troublesome disciplines of faith, prayer, study or ritual, no membership dues or charity pledges, no need to identify one's personal faith with the destiny of his people. The pagan can do anything he wants at any time—and it doesn't cost him money.

Liberal religion is in the intensely inconvenient position of trying to stand up and live between the lower millstone of the fundamentalists who are so sure of so many things that aren't so, and the upper millstone of the atheists or the pagans, who are so sure of their belief that they can't believe in anything.

Someone once remarked somewhat facetiously, "A Jew is just like any other person, only more so; and a Reform Jew is just like any other Jew, only less so." This may be untrue but it is not unjustified in the minds of some. All too many delude themselves into thinking that

Reform is a lesser brand of Judaism than its orthodox counterpart. How often one hears people say, "I am not as religious as my parents. I am a Reform Jew." Generally speaking, that person really means he is not as observant of the minute ceremonial customs and traditions; he is not as "fromm" or as pious about fulfilling the *mitzvot*.

Another notion about which we occasionally hear is that Reform Judaism gives a person the license to discard all Jewish values—"The less Jewish you are, the more Reform you are," etc. As if Reform Judaism authorizes a person to stay away from services constantly, to read no Jewish books or study no Jewish literature, to disassociate himself from all worthy Jewish causes, and otherwise lead a life devoid of any spiritual content! Such foolishness! Reform Judaism gives no such license to any Jew. To be sure, Reform Judaism lays less stress upon ceremonies and ritual, but those rituals and ceremonies which it does retain or modify are emphasized as strongly as possible. Reform Judaism calls for full participation. It insists on high educational standards. Convenient or not, it demands dignity and decorum, reverence and sincerity for the inner heart. Mere ignorance of orthodox Judaism does not qualify one to be a Reform Jew. Properly, a Reform Jew is one who is so well versed in the history and literature of Judaism that he is able to distill the essence of its teaching and able to translate it into daily life. The Reform Jew should be familiar with all aspects of historical Judaism. He should be the learned student who knows enough to separate essence from form. A person who is possessed of a burning idea is not content to keep it to himself. Reform Jews must teach the cardinal principles of Judaism to the members of their families, to other Jews, and ultimately, to non-Jews as well. Those who teach how life may be improved, it is said, are equal to those who create life. Thus, a Reform Jew is not one who practices less of Judaism than an orthodox Jew. The justification for shedding Jewish observance of much of its ceremony is that we shall then be able to devote our greater energy to the projection of the essence of Judaism, the moral law, into all avenues of life.

To do all this is no easy task. Rabbi Jacob J. Weinstein reminds us trenchantly, "Judaism has never been a faith for softies. It was and is a religion for tough-minded men. It offers no peace of mind but rather a divine discontent. It offers serenity only to those who earn it on life's battlefields." Judaism is not "kid-stuff" nor a lullaby to serenity. Judaism is not merely for children whose parents need one morning a week for sleep. It is for grown-ups who need to be awakened to their mature responsibilities as parents and as living examples to their children.

Is Reform Judaism just a religion of convenience? Some people think that it is so easy to be a Reform Jew (or for that matter, a conservative Jew!) and that it is much harder to be an orthodox Jew. Oh no! The reverse is true. Anyone can be an orthodox Jew by following the neatly prescribed rules and regulations. It is much harder to be a Reform Jew, intelligent and informed about Judaism, for he has to decide for himself on the basis of reading and study, discussion and commitment, what to retain of Judaism and what to reform and refashion. His is the responsibility to practice Jewish traditions that have meaning for him and his generation, not because it is commanded from "on high," but because in his heart and in his soul is the burning conviction that this is worthwhile for him. His is the responsibility to see the symbolism, the moral teaching behind the ceremony or ritual, and to carry out that ethical ideal in daily life; to practice what is preached; to fulfil the rabbinic injunction to "perfect the world under the sovereignty of God."

This is no lazy-man's approach to Judaism or Jewish life, but a sincere attempt to make Judaism real and meaningful to people. It demands sacrifices and disciplines, for no religious movement can long survive unless it has these from its followers.

The late Claude G. Montefiore of England used to say: "We Jews have a more pressing responsibility for our lives and beliefs than perhaps any other religious community! Don't shelter yourself in any course of action by the idea that 'it is not my affair.' It is your affair, but it is also mine and the community's. Nor can we neglect the world beyond. A fierce light beats upon the Jew. It is a grave responsibility—to be a Jew . . . *Ten bad Jews may help to damn us; ten good Jews may help to save us.* Which minyan will you join?"

"The Cult of Reassurance"

Easy? A religion of convenience? No, Judaism is hardly that. It is a religion for stout-hearted, great-souled men and women who want something more than the soothing syrup of pet nostrums about "making friends and influencing people" or "the power of positive thinking." It is a religion of need and deed, not creed and feed, that is making its appeals to third-generation American Jews who want to reclaim what their fathers, the second generation, rejected. They are not reclaiming the ghetto Jewish life of their grandfathers, associated with poverty and want, suffering and degradation and humiliation. What this third generation wants is rather a religion of content, a Judaism that makes the Bible and the Rabbinic treasures meaningful for our time, a Judaism rich in the millennial experience of our people, a Judaism that is relevant to our spiritual situation.

In 3,000 years, it has never been easy to be a Jew. Judaism is a religion for brave-hearted, tough-minded people. It offers not peace of mind, but Divine discontent over the problems of inequality, insecurity, poverty, misery, want—the basic problems that plague the families of the earth. Judaism pricks our conscience with the realization that tonight most people on this earth will go to sleep ill-fed, ill-clothed, ill-housed, enslaved by social or political or economic bondage that sooner or later must be broken. Judaism is not a religion of convenience that says you can lick a problem by ignoring it, or by pretending to overcome evil, or by pretending it doesn't exist. Judaism is not a religion of compulsive escapism into the never-never land where there are no problems, no human suffering, no social dislocations, no difficult decisions. Judaism is realistic! It faces life both as it is and as it ought to be.

Judaism never promises that it will wipe away all problems for the religious. Suffering and failure and trouble are part of life. These trials of the spirit come to everyone, even to a Jacob, a Moses, a Job. These things happen all the time in life. Sometimes people say to me, "What did *I* do to deserve such a fate? Why should this happen to *me,* of all people?" It seems almost futile to say to such a blind person, "These things happen all the time. You just never realized what goes on in the world around you. Yesterday it was your brother. Today it is you. It is not what happens to you that really counts. It's how you take it—how you meet the unexpected—that in the long run determines your character."

Judaism says something else in protest against the "cult of reassurance" as the new religion. This new religion seems only concerned with the individual and with his selfish search for happiness. Judaism is concerned with society. Judaism's prayer book is written in the syntax of the first person plural, not the singular. We lift up our voices in the Adoration:
dignity, justice and equality, mercy and lovingkindness to

> "Fervently we pray that the day may come when all men shall invoke Thy name, when corruption and evil shall give way to purity and goodness, when superstition shall no longer enslave the mind nor idolatry blind the eye, when all who dwell on earth shall know that to Thee alone every knee must bend and every tongue give homage . . ."

The Jewish way of life that speaks of the prophetic message, the mandate to build the Kingdom of God on earth. It is the voices of Amos, Isaiah, and their company, bidding us find the courage to apply the standards of decency and the problems of a world that must become one . . . one brotherhood of man under one Fatherhood of God. That is the millennial dream of Judaism's way of life. That is the Jewish heritage.

Seeking Commitment

Despite the current revival of religion, especially among the thoughtful third generation of American Jews, all is not well if only a religion of convenience is what is offered as authentic religious experience. Young people are not returning to that shallow a message of faith. They want —and are entitled to—something deeper, more soul-searching, than simply convenience. They want commitment.

They ask themselves—what is a religious person? Who is a religious man?

Rabbi Louis Binstock gives an answer worth pondering in *The Power of Faith:*

> A religious man is a Moses beholding a world filled with the slavery of his fellow men and refusing to remain free until his brothers have also been freed. A religious man is an Amos beholding a society reeking with injustice, and refusing to remain silent so long as the waters of justice are not permitted to flow like a clear and mighty stream. A religious man is an Isaiah beholding a world weltering in a blood bath of war, and refusing to rest so long as men have not yet learned to turn their swords into ploughshares and their spears into pruning hooks. A religious man is a Jesus beholding the tragic plight of the underprivileged and the overtaxed, and refusing to be silent until their burdens are lifted and their sorrows assuaged. A religious man is a Gandhi beholding lives filled with human degradation and oppression, and refusing to eat until the lowliest "untouchables" might enjoy all the advantages and opportunities of their ruling brothers. A religious man always, among every people and in every generation, is he whose soul is depressed by the ugliness and rottenness he finds smudging the canvas of life, and who insists upon painting it over with the brighter and lovelier colors of beauty and truth, freedom and justice, love and peace. In short, a religious man is one who has faith in the ultimate goodness of the universe. But a genuinely religious man is rare in our time. Hundreds of thousands belong to congregations, confess creeds, offer prayers. Only hundreds belong, confess and offer themselves to God. There is a vital distinction between having a faith (religion) and having faith. The one is, as a rule, only an outer form. The other is exclusively an inner spirit.

One is a religion of convenience. The other is a religion of commitment.

One is a faith in faith, the other is a faith in God.

Liberal Judaism pleads not for convenience, but for commitment, for conviction by means of sincere and whole-souled devotion to following the will of God. This alone will yield the quest for authentic religion in modern Judaism.

6. *MAKING A DECISION FOR JUDAISM*

Newspapers were full of reports recently of an amazing phenomenon going on in New York City. Billy Graham was taking over New York. Nightly his crusade jammed the Madison Square Garden. What he said there, how he said it, and to how many thousands of people, was reported day after day in front-page stories. Some thought his revival good, some thought it bad, but whatever people thought he put religion on the map in "irreligious New York."

Many Jews began saying, "What we need is a Jewish Billy Graham! We need a religious revival." Yet have you ever considered that we Jews hold a religious revival every year? We call this annual religious revival our High Holy Days. And we go not to any boxing arena or baseball park or tent with a sawdust trail, but to stately and beautiful synagogues and temples, there to worship God in the beauty of holiness.

Each night Billy Graham called upon his huge audience to repent. "Every one of you is a sinner," he would say. "You won't be saved unless you repent." Now, Judaism does not say that man is by nature depraved or that a man's soul must be saved by an act of Divine grace. In Judaism, repentance, *teshuva,* is a normal aspect of human life. We treasure a special season every year when we talk about sin and repentance. Beginning with Rosh Hashana and ending with Yom Kippur, Jews set aside ten days for intensive reflection and earnest prayer, not in hysterical evangelism, but in sober meditation and quiet solemnity.

Part of Billy Graham's crusade highlighted hundreds of Christians who came forward to the altar rail to make a climactic "decision for Christ." There is nothing analogous in Judaism to this form of public testimonial. Jews are not asked to make a "decision for Moses" or "for Judas Maccabeus" or for anyone else. Jews cannot, by hearing one shouting sermon about fire and brimstone, suddenly become steeped in Judaism. Ours is a life-long discipline that we call "the Jewish way of life." It is composed of learning and praying and doing. It is a matter of education, of worship, of identification, of participation, of applying the ethical teachings of Judaism into the practical affairs of daily life.

But Jews can make a "decision for Judaism." We can end indifference, the emptiness of our inner lives, by filling some of those empty hours with substance and meaning, with study and discussion of Jewish thought and Jewish problems. This kind of "decision for Judaism" can be our religious revival.

Years ago our synagogues and temples were smaller and simpler. There were fewer Jews in this country, but their fervent piety carried over into their homes and daily lives. Today, for all our magnificent synagogues and temples, with bigger memberships, bigger religious schools, bigger edifices, bigger budgets, there is much less carry-over into the lives and hearts of our people.

Jews in America are determined to survive as Jews. Their existence and identity are no longer open to challenge from within. Jews in America no longer feel that they need prove their Americanism by soft-pedaling or discarding their Judaism. There is no rush to conversion, no rash of assimilation, no dissolution in the processes of acculturation whereby the distinctive marks of the Jewish group are being dissolved, as has sometimes happened in periods of prosperity and freedom. On the contrary, just the reverse is taking place. There is more Jewish-mindedness today than a generation ago. Despite lush times with high incomes and full stomachs and new roofs over the heads of American Jews, despite the breakdown in educational barriers and quotas and fraternities, despite greater opportunity than ever before to mingle freely in the market places of business and professional life, the last twenty-five years have found American Jews going through a period of "agonizing reappraisal." A strong revival of Jewishness is going on in our time, an emphasis on identification and solidarity with the Jewish people at home and abroad. The revival of Jewishness is booming, of Jewish-mindedness, of Jewish spirit, of affiliation and identification with the Jewish destiny. But there is a sharp distinction between Jewishness and Judaism. One is a chauvinistic, emotional, sometimes nostalgic attachment to objects and people connected with secular Jewish culture. The other has to do with God, with the sacred and the holy. One is not the same as the other. One is not a substitute for the other.

Three Groups Being Drawn to Judaism

The revival of Jewishness, of identification with the Jewish people the world over, seems solid and strong. But the revival of Judaism, the spiritual aspects of the religious revival, seems open to many serious reservations. Several considerations are involved in the superficiality of this religious revival of Judaism.

One of these is the patriotic desire of Jews, like Christians, to escape from the imputation of Communism. In the mind of most American Babbitts, there is a close correlation between Communism and atheism. Anyone who does not believe in God is suspect. Atheism has become the trademark of the godlessness of Communism. Consequently, affiliation with a religious institution brings with it an aura of respectability and removes any doubts from their Christian or Jewish neighbors that they are fully American. It has become the American thing to do.

Still others have been persuaded to join a congregation because of inner loneliness and isolation, what might be called psycho-sociological necessities. For example, in many metropolitan areas like New York and Chicago, a wholesale flight to the suburbs has taken place among Jews who previously had little or no formal affiliation with religion. Yet when they arrive in suburbia they are drawn to association with other Jews out of sheer loneliness.

The third group of more sensitive souls is drawn to a "return to religion" because of fears in this atomic age. The disillusionment of many thoughtful people over the world's failure to find a rational solution to atomic war, to the arms race in guided missiles, to the East-West conflict, and the new global imperialism which both Russia and the United States have developed, have caused many people, including Jews, to review their basic thinking. Three successive decades of depression, world wars, mass murdering of six million of our people, the cynical indifference of the great powers to the plight of Israel, even the anxieties inherent in post-war prosperity, have turned many Jews to profound questioning. And they have come to the conclusion that the fundamental values of religion are what civilization now stands in frantic need of. They have found in Jewish thought, in Jewish prayer, in Jewish literature, in Jewish philosophy, a renewal for the aching spirit which so sorely troubles our time.

From Quantitative to Qualitative Experience

The real challenge to us, however, should not be the cynical question, "How come all this revival of Jewish interest in synagogues and temples?" Rather we need to examine the situation and ask, "How can we translate this religious revival so quantitatively impressive but so qualitatively shallow into something real and dynamic and meaningful? How can rabbis and thoughtful laymen together utilize the presence of large groups, especially younger people, and educate them about the role of religion in human affairs? What can the individual Jew do who is faced with his own problems of disappointment and heartache, who eagerly seeks bread for the famine of the human spirit?"

Here are three simple, very simple, suggestions. But like freedom or democracy or peace, it is much easier to outline the rules than to live them. Still, the fact that goals may be difficult to attain should not diminish our efforts to make real the ideal. These suggestions are:

1. *Make religion a way of life.* Religion involves primarily one's awareness of God and a person's relationship to Him, a continuing and enduring sense of God's presence in the universe. The Talmudic inscription over many a Holy Ark, reads, "Know before whom thou standest." When you know before whom you stand, when you pray not because it is fashionable or proper or socially desirable,

but because of an inner urge to commune with God, you then know what the Lord expects of you: "To do justly and to love mercy and to walk humbly before God." For such people, religion is a way of life. It teaches them to be just and righteous and compassionate because this is what God requires of a person.

People are continually saying in these benighted times, "I want solace."—"I need confidence."—"I'm looking for peace of mind."—"Can religion offer me these?"

Yes, but only as by-products of religion. A person who is truly and sincerely religious does find comfort and courage. The man who knows before whom he stands and strives to live in the presence of God is never alone. His spirit is strengthened, his soul is soothed, because in his hours of difficulty God is his source of strength.

You cannot turn on a Divine stream of strength the way you turn on a faucet when you're thirsty. Religion gives courage and strength to master adversity, but only when you've made it a habit. It is not like a bottle of aspirin, to take only when you have a headache. Such religion is no better than aspirin. It doesn't do much; it doesn't help much; it doesn't cost much; it isn't worth much. But when religion is a way of life, an on-going experience, a living reality; when religion is like the synagogue prayer recited each week from Deuteronomy, "When thou sittest in thy house, when thou walkest by the way, when thou liest down and when thou risest up," then religion becomes a guide, a fortress, a shield, a rock. Then, religion brings you not only into a relationship with God, its primary function, but its secondary by-products are attained as well: solace and comfort, courage and strength, confidence and hope. Making religion a way of life means living "The Ten Commandments of Religious Maturity" composed by Rabbi Norbert L. Rosenthal:

To thyself be true,
To thy family be affectionate,
To thy neighbor be generous,
To thy community be serviceable,
To mankind be just,
To every living creature be compassionate,
To the world be courageous,
To the past be understanding,
To the future be hopeful,
And to God be humble.

When you live those ten commandments of religious maturity, you have made religion a way of life.

2. *Study what Judaism is.* It's hard to follow the Jewish way of life if you don't know what Judaism is. Judaism has a message for today because it has lived through yesterday. What that message is, how it came to be and why it is powerfully relevant to our time needs to be understood by informed Jews. Fortunately in the last few years there has been a flood of books, magazines, pamphlets describing in various degrees of detail what Judaism really is. I commend them to your reading.

The gentle Hillel was once asked by a heathen to tell him the essence of Judaism while standing on one foot. Said Hillel, in his famous statement that is usually quoted only in part: "What is hateful unto thy neighbor do not do. This is the whole law, the rest is but commentary." What is usually omitted is Hillel's brief admonition, without which his familiar Golden Rule is sterile. Added Hillel wisely, "Now, go forth and study."

3. *Practice the principles of Judaism in daily life.* Judaism is like a healthy muscle. It needs exercise. If you don't use it, it withers. If you do, it becomes stronger and more powerful. To any athlete, to any musician, to any dancer, to any artist, to any surgeon, practice is crucial. Without practice each would go to seed. Is it any different

with religion? No, we must practice our Judaism if we want to keep in spiritual condition. How?

How to Practice Judaism

You practice your Judaism through prayer. You needn't feel bashful or self-conscious about praying to God. Whether it is in your home on the Sabbath or in the Temple at worship, you should regard prayer not as a means toward a magic answer for personal wants or special rewards, but rather "as a means of reaching your higher self and placing it in tune with the higher purposes of society and of the universe." We need to pray today. Prayer helps us realize that man-centered life is an illusion. Unless we realize the processes of God at work in human destiny operate in good times or bad, in war or at peace, we might be tempted (as some are vainly boasting today), "My power and the might of my hands have gotten me this wealth." The Union Prayerbook for the Sabbath service says to such a person, "But may we remember that it is Thou who givest strength to acquire substance. And may we bear in mind that Thou who givest canst also take away; and when Thou takest away, may we not have cause to reproach ourselves that we have not justly and wisely used Thy gifts.'

You practice your Judaism through your actions with others, with your fellow-men. Jewish ethics can be divided into two parts: our obligations to God and our obligations to the human race. The Talmud says that on Yom Kippur, God can only grant pardon for man's sins against God Himself. He cannot pardon man's sins against his fellowman until a person has made amends for them. Judaism has a proud record of dedicated concern for our fellow-men. It is written into thousands of laws and obligations and *mitzvot*. Today, the social action movement emphasizing the universal teachings of the prophets and their application to modern social problems conveys an indication of how zealously the leaders of Reform Judaism are striving to make the religious revival sincere and significant. Reform Judaism especially emphasizes the moral mandate to bring the ethics of Judaism into the highways and byways of life, to "apply prophetic precepts to the market place, to mine and mill, to street and slum, to factory and farm," in the words of Rabbi Maurice N. Eisendrath. But before doing this, we have to know where Judaism stands on these issues. What is the Jewish point of view on housing, on education, on marriage and the family, on delinquency, on civil rights, on church and state, on immigration, on world peace?

There is a definite Jewish tradition on each of these thorny problems. Take, for example, the gathering storm over segregation in America. Judaism has a definite stake in this issue. The Bible repeatedly said, "One law for the stranger and the homeborn shall there be." The prophet Amos said, "Are ye not unto Me as the Ethiopians, O children of Israel, saith the Lord." The Talmud said, "The law of the land is the law." Consequently, the open revolution against the law of the land, aided and abetted by elected officials of Southern states, has an added sting for American Jews. Not only as Americans are we zealous for the integrity and honor of our country, but as Jews we have a time-honored feeling that equality of educational opportunity, whether for black or for white, Christian or Jew, is fundamental to social justice. Desegregation is more than a political football. It is a moral and religious issue. We Jews deplore all efforts to frustrate and evade the decisions of the United States Supreme Court, whether directly or deviously. We Jews know from the bitter and grim experiences of our own people what it means to be denied opportunity, to be discriminated against because of bigotry, to be hated and hounded and harried by ignorant whites who are both un-Christian and un-American. There must be no second-class citizenship in America of privilege restricted to white Christians only—no second-class schools for colored children, no second-class passports for traveling in the Middle East, no second-class uniforms for our Air Force personnel stationed in Saudi Arabia.

This is sound Americanism. It is also sound Judaism.

Segregation is one more example of how Americans love democracy but hate to practice it. Many are the signs of retreat and discouragement which might momentarily frustrate us. The failure of the disarmament conference, the dangerous testing of nuclear weapons, the chipping away of foreign aid, the anemic, watered-down civil rights bills begrudgingly passed by Congress, the fuse in the Middle East powder keg kept dangerously lit by American bungling no less than by Soviet exploitation . . . oh, there are plenty of problems that frustrate us as individuals over the pull of world events. How inadequate we feel in the midst of the world's problems!

No wonder there is a hungering in our time for religion and for the message of religion. People are no longer as sure as they once were about ultimate questions. They feel a great emptiness. One college student said recently, "What's the use of playing the game if you don't know where the goal posts are?" Never before has there been a deeper need to believe in something greater and vaster than ourselves.

A "decision for Judaism" involves doing three simple things in the years ahead: 1. Make religion a way of life. 2. Study what Judaism is all about. 3. Practice the principles of Judaism in daily life. You may not save the world that way. What can? Who can? But you can add your little link to the mighty chain of human freedom that ultimately must bind together the whole human family.

PART II

TO SURVIVE AS JEWS

7. *ARE THERE TYPICAL JEWISH CHARACTERISTICS?*

EVERY HISTORY of the Jews ever written shows that at one time the Jewish people were persecuted because of the Church's religious fanaticism. Stubbornly and persistently, Jews refused to forsake their faith and accept Jesus as Lord or Savior. Chapter after chapter is stained with Jewish blood as the Inquisition sought to stamp out by force what it considered a religious heresy. There are countless stories about Jewish martyrs at the stake and on the rack who defied all the engines of torture devised by the Torquemadas of tyranny simply because they had an unwavering loyalty to Judaism.

In the nineteenth century a new name for an old hatred arose, called anti-Semitism. Jews were virulently opposed not because of their religion but because of their so-called race: they were thought to be Semites. With all the trappings of truth, the new movement against the Jews wrapped itself in a scientific cloak. Anti-Semites charged that Jews were an inferior race and should not be given the full rights of citizenship in a nation inhabited mostly by Aryans. They developed the myth of the "typical Jew" who was disgustingly caricatured by artists, cartoonists and penmen, diabolically ingenious. Hitler exploited this myth of the typical Jew to its fullest extent. We can still recall the Goebbels propaganda of the hook-nose, thick-lipped, avaricious Jew; the usurious Shylock, the loud, clannish, ostentatious displayer of newly acquired riches; the sharpster living on his wits, the middleman, the parasite, the "luftmensch . . ."

These slanders became identified by the Nazis as typical Jewish characteristics. Our detractors dinned them into the consciousness of unsuspecting Christians. Alas that some of our own Jewish people became contaminated with this overpowering poison of self-hate! Many of them heard the slanders so often that they began to believe them. That was the greatest tragedy of all . . . for when a man begins to think ill of himself, he can never stand up to the world. He is done for.

This is not the place to enter into the field of Jewish apologetics and explain how these erroneous and malevolent defamations became associated with the myth of typical Jews. Anthropologists have written volumes of scientific studies refuting the preposterous race theories of the anti-Semites about Jewish noses, pigmentation, configuration of the head, hair, lips and other anthropological criteria. The social psychologists have studied the charges of clannishness and ostentations. They understand that these are merely manifestations of Jewish insecurity brought on by the world's hostility; or longings for a sense of significance in the face of social frustrations. Historians have studied the role of the Jew in economics. They understand that Jews developed a commercial acumen in their struggle for survival simply out of sheer necessity. Prevented by the medieval feudal system from holding land or entering the trade guilds, they became barterers and lenders at the very time that the rise of the modern nation-state needed middlemen to provide capital to facilitate the free flow of goods and services. And here in the new world their hard work, daring imagination, and intense fidelity were the very qualities that the expanding American frontier needed. But again economic prejudices prevented Jews from entering certain fields of endeavor, and as the *Fortune* study showed a few years ago, Jews were herded into certain prescribed economic areas without their consent while other pastures were fenced off and Jews forbidden to trespass upon them. Yet despite the fact that anthropologists, psychologists, and historians can demonstrate scientifically that these so-called typical Jewish characteristics are either made of whole cloth or are the consequences of historical injustices, the myth of the typical Jew has nonetheless persisted. We miss the point entirely when we decry and deny that there are any typical Jewish characteristics. I believe that there are typical Jewish characteristics—only not the ones most people usually think of. These characteristics are to be found not in all who are born Jews, but they are found in nearly all who profess their affiliation and certainly in all who are what Jean Paul Sartre has termed "authentic Jews."

Attachment to Learning

The first characteristic that I would ascribe to Jews is their attachment to learning. The *beau ideal,* the honored man in Judaism, has always been the man of learning rather than the military leader or the politician or the rich. In Jewish tradition the title of *talmid chacham,* a disciple of the wise, represented the ultimate in social appreciation and recognition. In a world in which the homeless and driven Jew was forced by his enemies to become a despised huckster of material goods, he discovered by experience that learning was the only "merchandise" that had enduring value. It could neither be lost nor stolen nor snatched from him by violence, as in the case of his material chattels. Hillel once said, "He who does not seek to acquire wisdom forfeits his life." In Judaism the ideal of being learned was a religious virtue.

With the breakdown of ghetto life after the French Revolution and the weaning away of Jewish intellectuals from the exclusively Jewish circle, the Jew's attachment to learning shifted to secular and general areas of knowledge. But modern Jews have not forgotten their ancestors' attachment to learning. Today they regard it a primary obligation to give their children the best education possible, to send them to the best schools, to expose them to the best cultural influences calculated to develop character-building, to prepare them with the finest mental tools for making their livelihood. It is no accident that Jews have gravitated to the sciences and professions requiring advanced post-graduate studies. Through centuries of vicissitudes, attachment to learning has become a typical characteristic of the Jews—down to this very day.

Aversion to Violence

The second characteristic typically Jewish is aversion to violence. The gentle Hillel once counseled our people: "Be of the disciples of Aaron, loving peace and pursuing it." Peace as a social ideal goes back to prophetic times. When the prophets of Israel preached their message of universalism and spoke about the Fatherhood of God and the Brotherhood of Man, they were actually saying that when men act as brothers and treat each other as brothers, there will be peace. Throughout the centuries

Jews maintained and affirmed their devotion to the ideal of peace. The classic hope of the synagogue is the cherished prayer, "Grant us peace, Thy most precious gift, and enable Israel to be a messenger of peace unto the peoples of the earth . . ."

The teachers of Judaism recognized that the achievement of peace requires a type of social order from which the basic causes of group friction have been removed. Peace is the by-product of justice. The Talmud says: "The sword comes into the world because of justice being delayed, because of justice being perverted and because of those who render wrong decisions (averting justice)." In Judaism, the world movement for peace is therefore coupled with the movement for social justice. For as Hillel said, he who increases justice increases peace.

With the emergence of the modern nation-state and the emancipation of Jewry in western countries, Jews have shared with their fellow citizens of other faiths in all of the responsibilities of national defense. American Jews can be immensely proud of the heroic record of Jewish boys who served our country in time of war and who earned a distinguished record in the fight for human freedom. One should also be proud of the Jew's continuing ferment of dissatisfaction with a world which must periodically sacrifice the flower of its youth in the mad self-destruction of war. Jewish idealism for peace makes a powerful impact upon the Jew of today: he is taught the ways of peace from earliest childhood. Judaism is full of affirmations exalting the ideal of peace and aversion to violence. Recently I had occasion to look up the article on "Peace" in the *Universal Jewish Encyclopedia* and found lists of hundreds of statements culled from the Bible, Talmud, Midrash and modern advocates of peace. When we speak of typical Jewish characteristics, let this glorious ideal given to the world by ancient Israel not be forgotten! The world has risked much for war. Let it risk as much for peace! That thought is typically Jewish.

Humanitarian Concern for Fellow-Jews

The third noble characteristic which I would put on my list is our humanitarian concern with our fellow-Jews. Back in 1654 when Peter Stuyvesant was governor of the Dutch colony of New Amsterdam and 23 refugee Jews sought to be admitted there, Stuyvesant sternly stipulated one condition: that they were never to become a burden on the non-Jewish population and were to take care of their own poor. The Jews accepted that condition with alacrity because they had a tradition deeply ingrained within them of humanitarian concern for their fellow-Jews. And the Jews of America never went back on their word.

Since prophetic times charity has been the cornerstone of Jewish life. Charity was not considered a crumb to be thrown to the needy. There are two Hebrew expressions which are usually translated by the English word "charity" —the Biblical word *tsedakah* and the rabbinic phrase *gemilut chasadim. Tsedakah* comes from the Hebrew root meaning "justice" or "righteousness." *Gemilut chasadim* means "performing acts of lovingkindness." No word in the English language exactly conveys the meaning of *tsedakah.* Basic to *tsedakah* are religious, social and ethical implications that are fundamental to human relations. The Jewish tradition is that the poor have rights and the rich have obligations. From *tsedakah* developed the concept of *gemilut chasadim,* which the rabbis of the Talmud declared to be one of the three fundamental principles of the social order. "Upon three great principles is the world established," they said, "upon *Torah* (learning), upon *Avodah* (religious services or worship), and upon *Gemilut Chasadim* (acts of charitable lovingkindness)."

Modern times have witnessed a glorious chapter written in the history of Jewish charity. The Jewish community of America has erected great social institutions—welfare federations, hospitals, community centers, old folks' homes, and many other benevolent institutions—to take care of those whom ancient Scripture singled out for special protection: the widowed and the orphaned, the poor and the stranger within thy gates. The present generation of American Jewry has developed a technique of collecting charity money wholly unprecedented in private philanthropy. How else could the remnant of our people be redeemed from the prison camps of Europe? How else could embattled Israel struggling for her very survival take in over one million Jews in her first decade of existence, but for the fact that she could count on one typical Jewish characteristic: *Jews know how to give!*

Integrity of Family Relationships

In many ways the greatest source of Jewish strength is the home—the fourth characteristic. Many of the influences most lasting in our life were implanted in early childhood. During long centuries of Jewish suffering, the Jewish home became the one place in which the Jew could find dignity as a human being and peace in the midst of trouble. However the world treated him outside, however crushed he was elsewhere, in his own home the Jew straightened his back and stood erect as a man and as a son of God.

Heine once wrote: "The Jewish home was a haven of rest from the storms that reached round the very gates of the Ghetto and made a fairy palace in which the bespattered objects of the mob's derision threw off their garb of shame and assumed the royal attire of free men. The home was the place where the Jew was at his best . . . in the home he was himself!"

Yet, the Jew's home was rarely his "castle." It was something far higher—his sanctuary. In a special sense Judaism is a religion of the home. Many beautiful customs center about the home, which not only teach our children the meaning of Judaism in terms of their own experience but also add color and warmth, joy and beauty.

To a greatly underestimated degree, Jewish life was preserved by the Jewish home. The result was that the Jewish family was drawn closer together. Here thrived the unit of solidarity and survival. High standards of morality and fidelity brought dignity and purity to the Jewish family. Jews were not, however, immune to the tensions and problems which focused on the family. On the whole, considering the statistics on divorce, delinquency, prison records, the moral integrity of Jewish family relationships makes this a typical Jewish characteristic of which Jews can be rightfully proud!

The Ideal of Religious Devotion

The fifth Jewish characteristic is one that has never failed the Jew in the long, bitter centuries: his devotion to the religion of Judaism. Whatever calamity befell him, the Jew's religious faith sustained him; his ethical standards upheld him.

Now you may think it strange to label "religious devotion" a typical trait of the Jew at a time when so many Jews are apparently irreligious, or at least indifferent to religious values. All modern Jews are not religious, although they are more religious than they think. Some people throw away a bushel of truth because it contains a grain of error, while others swallow a bushel of error because it contains a grain of truth. But even if you should grant for the moment that many, even most of them, are not devotedly religious, you would not admit that they have given up their religious faith. Other influences may have come into their life, crowding religion and the synagogue into a less central position than they once occupied. Yet not for a moment does an authentic Jew say today that this religious devotion to Judaism is unimportant. Witness the overflowing crowds who irresistibly return to the synagogue on the High Holy Days! Recall the compelling magnet which drew Jewish boys in service during World War II to a Rosh Hashana service or a Passover Seder, no matter how many miles they had to tramp in mud and rain! We Jews have not given up our ideal of devotion to Judaism —not by a long shot!

The trouble is that there is a gap between the ideal and real. We just don't come up to where we would like to be. Yet neither does America fulfil its ideals on civil rights the way it ought to. Does that mean that America has forsaken its ideals of guaranteeing every citizen his constitutional rights? America is still characterized as the last, best hope of the world, where every citizen has the right to enjoy the privileges of his "four freedoms." The tremendous gap between ideals and reality does not make us

Americans repudiate our ideals or discount them. Instead, we are impelled to work harder in translating them into daily values.

So it is with religious devotion as a Jewish characteristic. We Jews have not done all we can or should for Judaism. But neither have we given up our religion or forsaken our ideals. Deep down in our hearts is still the compelling voice of conscience. The word "ought" remains firmly lodged there.

The Miracle of Jewish Survival

So you see, detractors and defamers of the Jews are right on one point: we Jews do have typical characteristics—but not the slanders that have been spread about. The miracle of Israel's survival through forty centuries is pragmatically explained by a different approach to Jewish history. The Jew's attachment to Torah and learning, his aversion to violence, his love of peace—how else do you think the majority of Jews could have resisted apostasy and flight from Judaism if the Jewish home had not solidified unbreakable ties of loyalty and fidelity within the family? For what else has the Jew "suffered the slings and arrows of outrageous fortune" save to worship God in the Jewish tradition and practice his religion as he sees fit? These five qualities are typically Jewish. They are no freaks of fortune. They are the consequences of four thousand years of Jewish history. They link us, every one of us with a majestic past. Because of this heritage, the Jew of today can go back through the centuries and identify with himself the immortals who forged these qualities on the anvil of history.

As long as the Jew is faithful to the heritage developed

over the centuries—a heritage that includes such Jewish characteristics as love of learning, aversion to violence, humanitarian concern with our fellow-man, integrity of family relationships, the ideal of religious devotion—as long as these qualities endure, the Jew will live on as a link in an eternal chain. So may it be!

8. *WHAT MAKES BEING A JEW SO WORTHWHILE*

Some parents who have their hands full with teen-age adolescents may look a little askance at their various youth groups and say, "What is a youth group? A youth group is a bunch of kids who are never on time . . . who sit like babies unless you treat them as adults . . . who can't seem to settle down because one of them is tossing a bean bag, and one is doodling with your new fountain pen and all of them are chewing gum as if the world depended upon some saccharine secretion of saliva . . . while you are trying to get them to prepare something they had solemnly promised to do six and a half weeks ago, but had forgotten. A youth group is a gang of youngsters whose world seems to revolve about a basketball game, a date, a comic book, a piece of gum . . . who insist on telling you jokes that weren't funny when you were a teenager. A youth group is a conspiracy, sworn to the sacred task of driving you insane, by changing the subject, by forgetting appointments, and by giggling. And yet, when they turn to you for advice; when they speak of their goals in life; when they struggle to find expression for the beauty and the greatness and the sympathy and the dedication for which they yearn; when they come through with flying colors (as they always do) they cause a tingle to run up and down your spine, because you have, by holding their hands and their hearts, peeked into the future. You like what you see."

One reason I am so enthusiastic about the future of Reform Judaism's youth program is because of what it is doing to help make being a Jew seem worthwhile. So many young American Jews throughout the country find nothing worth living for in their Judaism. To them, being a Jew means being kept out of medical schools and eastern universities because of a Jewish quota. To them, being a Jew means being refused admission to some swanky resort. It means being prevented from living in certain apartment houses or from buying homes in certain restricted neighborhoods. It means being disqualified from getting a job in certain industries or entering certain professions. And before very long these Jews in name only succumb to feeling unwelcome, in some way undesirable and unacceptable because of a "gentleman's agreement." They are aware only of the irritating disadvantages of being a Jew. They know little or nothing of the positive affirmations that make being a Jew worthwhile. They share few of the pleasurable experiences identified with living as an American Jew. Integration of personality, balanced adjustment to the American environment of religious diversity, cultivation of Jewish self-respect and responsibility—these are outside the ken of such Jews.

If I thought that they were numerically insignificant, perhaps I would be less concerned with the problem of Jews without Judaism. I would think: Well, in every generation there are Jews who fly off the wheel of life and disappear like sparks in the night, leaving the *Shearith Yisrael,* the saving remnant, to carry on survival. But I am concerned because I find great numbers of Jews in metropolitan cities, especially among Reform Jews, who have little or no conception of Judaism and who associate being a

Jew only with the burdensome disabilities of persecution, defamation and discomfort.

I am convinced that one of the most disturbing problems to the modern American Jew is how to understand the worthwhileness of being a Jew—how to feel that the penalties and sacrifices demanded of Jews these days are worth bearing; how to maintain Jewish morale and psychological balance despite the freighted rumblings of a disturbing world. To know ourselves as Jews, to accept ourselves, to live with ourselves, is the crux of the problem of Jewish survival in America. Otherwise, why struggle so desperately and against such overwhelming odds to achieve survival—if we don't know what to do with it or how to live with it once won!

That so many young Jews who have everything in life ahead of them have failed to find the answer of living happily with their Judaism, is testimony to the urgency of this disquieting problem. Some Jews are not just human beings but constantly at war with their inner selves. They have found that they can't escape the battle. Subterfuge, false identity, and chameleon tactics are of no avail. Sooner or later, sailing under false colors is discovered. No corner of the globe is sufficiently remote to conceal their identity, not even hide-outs in distant rural places. So face the problem they must! And in facing it, such Jews are nervously "quaking in their boots." They do not have the spiritual armor to fight the battle with themselves. The result is that we have many dwarfed, neurotic Jews, frustrated by a sense of inadequacy and feeling of guilt, bowed down by the world's judgment of inferiority and unworthiness, jittery and jumping at the shadows of passing events.

Exaggerated? Overstated? Hardly!

No more challenging problem faces the leadership of American Israel—the rabbis, educators and lay leaders—

than to bring to coming generations of American Jewry a sense of worthiness and a feeling of spiritual security, an appreciation of Jewish values and ideals which alone can make survival a worthwhile achievement. What, then, are the values of Judaism that make being a Jew such a worthwhile, healthy-minded, spiritually satisfying experience these days? What can we find in Judaism for life that will bring us confidence in ourselves and courage for our destiny?

The Theology of Judaism

The first great positive value that makes being a Jew so worthwhile is the theology of Judaism—the beliefs, ideas and philosophy of our religion. Now, theology, though once regarded as the "queen of the sciences," is not the most popular subject in this atomic world. Some academic discipline is required to wind in and out of theology's labyrinth. Bernard Heller points out in his *Odyssey of a Faith* that Judaism is often described as a religion with a minimum theology. Yet a number of great principles, ideals that affect our lives deeply, stand out in the structure of Jewish theology—ideas that make sense and give intellectual responsibility to the thoughtful Jew.

Judaism holds that this universe of ours, with its immensities, its marvels, its bewildering pageant of the skies, did not happen by itself. It is not a colossal automatic engine of matter and force, mechanistic in operation, without direction or intelligence. Blind chance did not determine nature's laws of harmony. No, Judaism maintains that the universe was created by a cosmic Master of the world whom we call "God" . . . who is one, not two as

Zoroastrianism teaches, not three as Christianity teaches, but described unto Israel of old amidst the paganism and pantheons of Canaan, Egypt, Assyria, Babylonia, Persia, Greece and Rome: Look here, O Israel, the Lord *our* God is One!

Jewish theology further teaches that every man is created in the Divine Image as a child of God. That means that one God is the Father of all men, and all His children are brothers, endowed with moral freedom to choose between right and wrong . . . not burdened by any original sin, not bowed down with any sense of guilt, not predestined like some cosmic marionettes who move and act by the jerks of strings from on high. Judaism affirms that man can make his own moral choices. He has the freedom to cultivate the supremely distinctive quality of moral man—choosing right instead of wrong.

Without going into an exhaustive theological treatment of Judaism's belief about God and the nature of man,[1] let me submit that the theology and beliefs of Judaism are soundly convincing to the thoughtful Jew, and form one of the imperishable treasures to which Jews fall heir. The religion of Judaism, the theology of Judaism, the philosophy of Judaism make being a Jew a worthwhile privilege. To be a Jew without understanding what our faith believes in or stands for is like a ship without ballast. Even in calm seas, steering a straight course without listing is difficult, and when storms come and high seas break over the bow, the ship flounders. So it is with Jews without Judaism: they flounder and send up distress signals because

[1] See Abba Hillel Silver's *Where Judaism Differs* and Milton Steinberg's *Anatomy of Faith* for more detailed summation of the distinctive theological positions of Judaism. Steinberg's chapter, "New Currents in Religious Thought," pp. 214–300, sums up Christian influences on current Jewish theology.

they have no inner ballast to give them direction or security.

The Observances of Judaism

The second positive value in Judaism that makes being a Jew so worthwhile is its cluster of customs, ceremonies and practices. These give much joy and color to living as an American Jew. These observances emphasize the happy moments of life and give an air of festivity and joyfulness to an otherwise drab existence. Alas, there is all too much sorrow in the world today, and sometimes it is difficult to retain any serenity of spirit before the forces of hatred, selfishness, jealousy or greed. Proportion easily vanishes in the face of perilous times. But this is all the more reason for keeping our sense of balance! All the more reason for emphasizing the occasions that build morale and deepen the roots of psychological security. Our Jewish festivals and days of gladness bring many such opportunities, particularly in the home. I think of Passover when those families fortunate enough to have a Seder at home rejoice in this annual family reunion. They reread the story of the Haggadah and entertain the children's delight with the search for the Aphikomen. I feel sorry for those families who don't catch this spirit of joyous redemption and family festivity with a home Seder. I pity the children whose parents are too indifferent, too pseudo-sophisticated, to understand the meaningful pageantry of the Passover Seder.

The same thrill of family rejoicing is present at Hanukkah, when those parents who are sufficiently interested in their children's spiritual nurturing encourage the lighting of the Hanukkah candles. Exchanging gifts for Hanukkah and bringing a spirit of radiant happiness to the family circle makes it easier for the Jewish child to accept his Jewishness happily. Otherwise, he merely associates being a Jew with being deprived of a Christmas tree.

Or again, listen to the laughter at Purim time when the children come to religious school in masquerade costumes, some dressed as Mordecai, some as Esther. See the gleam in their eyes as they watch a Purim play and rejoice in the never-tiring tale of how justice ultimately wins out!

These are just some of the happy associations both at home and in the religious schol that linger in the memory of Jewish children. Later on in life, they will meet plenty of ugliness, plenty of distorted canards and lies that gnaw at the hearts of the Jewish people! If these are *all* the associations with being Jewish that a person has, then being a Jew is a pretty ugly experience. But when one is fortified with happy memories of home life as a child, when one feels secure in having experienced meaningful joys of Judaism from his youth on, he can take the bumps and knocks of later life in stride. He has been prepared. He has been forearmed.

How often I have seen Jews utterly bewildered by the anti-Semites' challenge to their security! How spiritually bankrupt they are when they have no balance on hand accumulated during the years of inner defense, of positive pride and sense of worth! I submit that there is much in Judaism, much in our holidays, customs and culture, much in our art, music and drama, to stabilize morale, to identify happy associations with Jewish life, to give us dignity and pride and a sense of worth. All of these help to make being a Jew worthwhile.

The Prophetic Spirit of Judaism

Now, a third positive value in our Judaism.

Some religions are more concerned with getting ready for the *next* life than they are with improving *this* life. They abandon hope for ameliorating economic and social conditions in this world and preach that salvation will come in the after-life. By abandoning any this-worldly ideal, they depreciate the significance of social situations right here. "When you get to Paradise in the next world," they argue, "what difference will it make if you have had to live in slums, suffer injustice, struggle with poverty, endure exploitation, or be deprived of life's good things? Get ready for the world to come, and just endure what you must in this life!"

Judaism protested against making religion a soothing opiate to deaden the pains of life on earth. Judaism affirmed in the spirit of the prophets that religion spurs men on in the battle against privilege, power and reaction. Religion acts as a catalytic agent, accelerating man's search for the good life. What will happen in the next world will be faced then, but here and now, says Judaism, man's primary duty is to perfect the world under the sovereignty not of the state, not of the class, but "under the sovereignty of God." Judaism teaches that working for international peace here on earth, for justice between nations and amongst men, for a more equitable distribution of the world's resources for the decencies of life, are religious concerns. And until there is fair dealing between man and man, until nations learn to bring equality of opportunity to all, our broken civilization on this earth will remain a tortuous denial of God's will.

That is Judaism, and that is why Judaism is so concerned with the social outlook of man, with his program for social justice, and social vision. The Bible is full of this message. The prophets, beginning with Elijah, Nathan and Amos, thundered it forth, and later prophets gave these jewels of justice a sublime setting:

> Seek justice, relieve the oppressed.
> —Isaiah 1:17

> Execute ye justice and righteousness, and deliver the spoiled out of the hand of the oppressor; and do no wrong, do no violence. —Jeremiah 22:3

> Is not this the fast that I have chosen?
> To loose the fetters of wickedness,
> And to let the oppressed go forth,
> And that ye break every yoke?
> —Isaiah 58:6

Prophetic idealism is no dead hangover from the past. It sets a moral standard in modern situations. It gives moral direction to the social advance in our day. Contemporary Judaism's social outlook stresses wages and hours, conditions of labor, collective bargaining, social security for the aged, the sick, the jobless, the widowed; public provision for health, housing, education and recreation; prevention of unemployment, abolition of child labor, birth control, preservation of civil liberties, removal of discrimination against people because of color, creed or place of birth, and the pursuit of something higher than sheer revenge in handling those who violate the law. Judaism means an informed opinion—not a deeply inflamed public opinion.

This is what Judaism means by applying the prophetic

mandate for social justice to the problems of *this* world. This is social action. This is *Judaism for life*—for the concerns and dislocations of life, for the worries and obstacles of life. That humanity must remain forever betrayed, plundered, profaned and disinherited, is intolerable even to those upon whom life has smiled. A social conscience is indispensable to the religion of Judaism.

In emphasizing a liberal social outlook, Judaism does not deny the importance of personal religion or belittle the need for the individual to attune man with the great moral and spiritual purposes of the Universe. The healing value of inner contemplation is copiously encouraged in the Bible and the Prayerbook. From the Psalmist and the Prophets, through Hillel, Akiba and Johanan ben Zakkai, from later rabbis and mystics and from Israel's seers and sages, an accumulated spiritual wisdom has been slowly gleaned and culled into a body of what Rabbi Joshua Loth Liebman once called "tested truth for man's moral guidance and spiritual at-homeness in the universe." There is plenty of opportunity within Judaism for individual fulfillment and personal uplift.

Still, man does not live in a vacuum. His daily life is not hermetically sealed. Judaism offers a prescription of ethical precepts to cover situations of social conflict. Judaism is not a weather vane swinging in a different direction with every puff of wind, but a guide post anchored securely to point the direction to the weary traveler. It offers a measuring rod of moral standards to help man live with his fellow-men. It offers a spirit that, when caught and applied to the vexing problems of life, is *dynamic,* charged with kinetic energy, a veritable transformer of latent spiritual power. With this kind of social program, Judaism has much with which to inspire men who are concerned with community betterment. The social outlook of Judaism for life, then, is the third great positive value that adds immeasurably to the worthfulness of being a Jew.

The Positive Values of Judaism

There are many other positive values of Judaism to mention—the glory of Jewish history and the matchless heroism of other generations . . . the concept of Torah and the implications of its all-embracing connotations . . . the idea of Israel and what kinship with the Jewish people means to the Jew of today . . . the place of prayer in Judaism . . . ideals of devotion, learning and piety . . . family solidarity and sanctification of Jewish home life. These and many more positive values are all to be found in the well springs of Judaism for those who will drink at its fountain.

To multiply illustrations is unnecessary. The point is that at a time of disillusionment and misfortune, thoughtful Jews who are disturbed over their Jewishness are thirsting for waters of healing. And it is becoming increasingly clear that there are no substitutes in Jewish life for Judaism. As Rabbi Abba Hillel Silver observes in his book, *The World Crisis and Jewish Survival,* neither philanthropy nor culture nor nationalism is adequate for the stress and challenge of our lives. All these interests can and must find their rightful place within the generous pattern of Judaism. But the pattern must be Judaism, the Judaism of the Bible, the Talmud and the Prayerbook, the Judaism of the priest, the prophet, the saint, the mystic and the rabbi, the Judaism which speaks of God and the worship of God and the unfathomable purposes of God and the eternal quest of God. Our people, and more especially our youth, require more than the example of generosity towards our unfortunate brothers overseas or a valiant defense of Jewish rights at home. They require a sense of security and at-homeness that comes from appreciating what they have in Judaism. Not that they should go around thumping their chests and proclaiming with arrant chauvinism, "I'm a Jew and I'm proud of it!" Too many are saying that with no idea at all of what they have a right to be proud. But to find a measured appreciation, to study and learn and then to live, to grasp its meaning for troubled times and apply its teachings towards making a better society, to gain a balanced evaluation of the worthfulness of being a Jew . . . that is finding Judaism for life. To paraphrase a little poem I love so well:

So give to Judaism,
Give to Jewish life and Jewish hope,
The best that you have—
And the best will come back to you!

9. *WHAT IT TAKES TO BE A JEW*

What does it take to be a Jew—a good Jew, a dedicated Jew, a believing Jew, one worthy of the name and proud history which 3,000 years have fashioned? I would like to describe the triangle of Judaism, and suggest that the three legs of this equilateral triangle constitute the symbol of our reply. Picture a large blackboard and draw the first line of the triangle.

A Mind

What does it take to be a Jew? It takes a *Mind*—a good, well-trained, educated mind. Judaism is not a religion for illiterates. The ideal of learning has been zealously fostered through a hundred generations of our people, because Judaism demands intellectual support of reason and logic. Blind faith, superstitious credulity—these are not enough.

To be sure, some religions are content to rest their authoritative hold on the people's unquestioning belief. But not Judaism. Irrational mysticism so popular in some neo-orthodox religious philosophies today has come and gone in Judaism. And in the process of give and take, Judaism has created a whole literature—the Bible, the Talmud, the Prayerbook, books of philosophy, history, theology, law.

Only the trained, eager mind can understand and appreciate this body of Jewish literature and thought, the greatness of Jewish literature, the inspiration of sacred books, the wisdom of prophets, psalmists, lawgivers and rabbis.

A Heart

Now note a second leg in our spiritual triangle. What does it take to be a Jew? It takes a *Heart.* The greatness of Judaism is that it is not all intellect and reason. Reform Judaism is only belatedly discovering this elementary truth that religion has to do with emotion as well, with warmth in religious experience. There are ceremonies and customs that enhance living, occasions in the life-cycle of the Jew that add richness and meaning, holidays and festivals that differentiate the sacred from the profane and raise man from the level of the brute.

Then, too, flowing in the blood stream pumped through the body of the Jew by this heart is the quality of mercy. The Jew's warm-hearted pulse beats not just for his own body but for others. Charity has been stressed in Jewish life because since Biblical times, when we were bidden to care for the "stranger, the widow and the orphaned," we Jews have developed a family feeling of one for the other. We have learned to take care of each other, to look after each other, to respond generously and graciously when our people have been in need, in sickness, in tragedy or in trouble.

This spirit of togetherness means that when one Jew is beaten, others feel it too. The buckshot of hate and prejudice fired by anti-Semites has pierced the heart of the Jew, making him especially sensitive to discrimination, bigotry, intolerance or abuse, whether directed solely at the Jew or at other minorities. Through bitter experience we have learned that once the poisoned arrows of venom are shot forth, they strike a multitude of targets; and the strong winds of prejudice and bigotry scatter them in all directions. Yes, it takes a strong and courageous heart to be a Jew today.

A Jew needs a heart, binding him to the Jewish people, a heart that must beat in time as one heart-throb with the hopes and aspirations of the Jewish people whether here in America, or in Israel, or in any of the far-flung corners of the globe where Jews seek to live in security and peace.

A Soul

Now the third leg of our triangle, and appropriately enough, the base on which the other two legs stand: what does it take to be a Jew? It takes a *Soul.*

Being a Jew requires a will to be a Jew. It involves a unique quality, a spiritual experience, that is the very essence of being a Jew.

For what else has the Jew survived and withstood the power of time, fortune and defeat, but to worship God in the Jewish tradition, to be part of the great Jewish heritage, to participate in the life and culture of our people as a self-respecting person?

And the essence of this religious experience? Prayer! Worship! Religious identification! Alas, there are other voices in Jewish life loudly clamoring for priority—nationalists, chauvinists, secularists, Yiddishists, assimilationists. But our commitment as Jews must be neither to the state nor the class nor the checkbook variety of Judaism. Our commitment belongs unto God. Our loyalty to Judaism is symbolized by the synagogue, the temple, as the institution of sacred associations.

Here, then, in this little triangle you find the symbol of the spiritual anatomy of the Jew—Mind, Heart and Soul. Many learned men have sought to define what it takes to be a Jew. The great Russian writer Tolstoy once gave this answer in a recently discovered letter in which he tried to answer what is a Jew:

> The Jew is that sacred being who has brought down from heaven the everlasting fire and has illumined with it the entire world. He is the religious source, spring and fountain out of which all the rest of the peoples have drawn their beliefs and their religions.
>
> The Jew is the pioneer of liberty. Even in those olden days, when the people were divided into but two distinct classes, slaves and masters—even so long ago had the law of Moses prohibited the practice of keeping a person in bondage for more than six years.
>
> The Jew is the pioneer of civilization. Ignorance was condemned in olden Palestine more even than it is today in civilized Europe. Moreover, in those wild and barbarous days, when neither the life nor the death of anyone counted for anything at all, Rabbi Akiba did not refrain from expressing himself openly.
>
> The Jew is the emblem of civil and religious toleration. "Love the stranger and the sojourner," Moses commands, "because you have been strangers in the land of Egypt." And this was said in those remote and savage times when the principal ambition of the races and nations consisted in crushing and enslaving one another . . . of such a lofty and ideal religious toleration not even the moralists of our present day can boast.
>
> The Jew is the emblem of eternity. He whom neither slaughter nor torture of thousands of years could destroy, he whom neither fire nor sword nor inquisition was able to wipe off the face of the earth, he who was the first to produce the oracles of God, he who has been for so long the guardian of prophecy and who transmitted it to the rest of the world—such a nation cannot be destroyed. The Jew is everlasting as is eternity itself.[1]

[1] Cited by Joseph L. Baron, *Stars and Sand,* p. 45.

10. *WHAT EVERY JEW SHOULD KNOW*

Ever since the time of Moses, the sages of Israel have known that only when Jews understand and devote themselves to Judaism can they be assured of life. There is an old legend that tells about Moses descending from Mount Sinai with the two tablets of the Law. Engraved on the stone tablets were the Divine Commandments of God. Such was the virtue of the inscription that it was not Moses who carried the tablets but the tablets which carried Moses. So it came to pass that his descent over jagged rocks and yawning chasms was effortless and safe. But when the prophet neared the foot of the mountain and caught a glimpse of the golden calf, when God's word and the idol were confronted with each other, a wonder ensued. The sacred letters detached themselves from the stone on which they had been inscribed and vanished into the thin mountain air. Moses was left holding a blank, inert thing, too heavy for him. Moses did not actually hurl the tablets to the ground, say the sages, and shatter them in rage. What actually happened was that he had to let them go or be crushed under their tremendous weight. The lettered tablets which once carried Moses were, once letterless, too much for him to bear.

It is not too difficult to discern what the ancient rabbis

were saying in their parable. Given knowledge and insight, Judaism sustains the Jew. Without it, being a Jew is a crushing burden, too heavy a burden to bear.

The Four C's of Judaism

Obviously, every Jew should know something of his religion. Now all religions that have long histories have four characteristics in common that begin with the letter "c": All historic religions have a) *a creed,* i.e. a body of beliefs, doctrines, or principles; they have b) *a code of conduct,* a body of ethical obligations growing out of a person's religious commitment; they have c) *a cult,* a body of organized ritual, practices and ceremonies which symbolize dramatically and forcefully that religion's ideals; and they have d) *a congregation,* a social bond uniting into one community or church or synagogue all who adhere to those particular beliefs, obligations and rituals.[1]

Judaism has all four of these "c's." We have a creed of beliefs that have gone through stages of progressive development for 4,000 years. To be sure, this cannot be regarded as a formalized doctrinal creed, but rather a group of principles of theology and ethics which form the Jewish idea of God and the nature of man.

We Jews have a code of conduct. The Torah has always been regarded as the source of our guiding law. And when times changed and the laws of the ancient Five Books of Moses no longer were socially applicable, new laws—the oral law, the *Mishna* and *Gemarah,* the *Talmud* and *Shulchan Aruch,* developed to direct the daily actions by which men should live. In all these codifications of Jewish practice,

[1] See Samuel S. Cohon, *What the Jews Believe,* p. 22.

the spirit of the Torah was the spirit of the Prophets. Those ancient men of God first perceived the connection between right living and right worshipping. Before the time of Amos and Isaiah and Jeremiah, all that counted was how men bowed down before the deity with sacrifices. How they lived seemed of no account. But from their time on, dignity, decency, justice, mercy and fairness were injected into the Jewish code of conduct. Today, our religious ethics maintain that not *for* p-r-o-f-i-t-s but *by* p-r-o-p-h-e-t-s shall man live with his neighbor. Said Zechariah: "Not by might and not by power but by my spirit, saith the Lord, shall man prevail."

Our religion also has a cult—that body of holidays, festivals, ceremonies, rituals, practices, and customs that distinguish Jewish worship, Jewish piety and Jewish living. These have been carefully developed through the ages. The Union Prayerbook used in Reform Jewish Temples throughout North America is the result of 2,000 years of creative thinking by the psalmists, sages, teachers, and rabbis. It is like a loose-leaf notebook of pious prayers reflecting the hopes and aspirations of each generation.

And finally, the Jewish religion centers in a congregation—the synagogue or temple which unites the families of Jewry into a single community. The social bond that ties one Jew to another, no matter from where he comes nor what language he speaks, is one of the unique phenomena of the world's history. No other religious fellowship has ever matched the Jewish spirit of world brotherhood.

Every Jew should know something about these four "c's"—*creed, code of conduct, cult and congregation*—which form the ingredients of Judaism.

Something About His Bible

As part of the Jewish religion, every Jew should know something about *his* Bible. I say "his" because the Bible is the personal possession of every Jew. Our forefathers gave it to the world. The world honors us for that gift. It behooves us, then, to know something about our patrimony for it is the textbook of our religion.

Rabbi Mortimer J. Cohen has written a little pamphlet, *How to Read Your Bible,* as a guide for Jewish soldiers and sailors. This is what he says: "It is the main source of our religion. It is the treasure house of our ethical teachings. From its pages all mankind has come to know that God is the Power that makes for justice, truth, and freedom in the world. Its spirit is intertwined with the roots of American democracy. Its greatest vision and hope for the future is a united world dedicated to universal justice and peace."

The Spirit of the Jewish People

Finally, every Jew should know something about his people—the Jewish people. We are a unique people, an *am s'gulah,* as the Bible puts it, a treasured people.

Jules Saint-Hilaire, the French Minister of Foreign Affairs during the Thiers cabinet, once said: "No people in the world has presented such a vivid example of unwavering perseverance and unflinching devotion to faith as the Jewish people. No nation has exerted so mighty a religious influence on humanity as Israel . . ."[1]

The idea of Israel (not the State of Israel, which is a new phenomenon that has reversed 2,000 years of Jewish life throughout the world) but the *concept of Israel as a living people* consists, in Mordecai M. Kaplan's words, of "generations of individual men and women who feel bound together by memories of a common past, by a fraternal feeling and desire to be responsible for one another and to perpetuate the most sacred of their historic memories, and by faith in the future significant role of the Jewish people in the life of mankind."

Each individual Jew is a member of the Jewish group. He looks to the group to give him faith, to help give meaning to his life, courage and guidance for living; the group looks to the individual to give loyal support to those institutions and those ways of living on which the very life of the group depends.

Every Jew who knows something about his people and his people's history has a right to take pride. One hundred and fifty unbroken generations of matchless faith, of creative thinking, of devotion to liberty, of perseverance against tyranny, of heroism and martyrdom, of unconquerable spirit!

Our religion!

Our Bible!

Our people!

Such are only three aspects about which every self-respecting American Jew ought to know something.

[1] Quoted by Joseph L. Baron, *Stars and Sand,* p. 86.

11. *HOW TO BE HAPPY AS A JEW*

Several years ago there appeared a revealing book by John Knight called, *The Story of My Psychoanalysis.* It was absorbing reading not simply because it was an excellent description of the various techniques involved in psychoanalytic treatment, but also because the author, an unhappy and bewildered research chemist, frankly disclosed the varying reactions to past events in his life which produced inner tension, conflicts, ulcers and collapse. What intrigued me the most in this book was the element of Jewishness which stood out as the vital quality in the make-up of this young chemist, his relationship with non-Jews, his attitudes toward being a Jew, his inner conflict over his Jewish past.

Jewishness is imbedded, in greater or lesser degree, in the personality context of all Jews. We must come to terms with it if we are to be happy, healthy-minded Jews. John Knight had not learned that. His analyst said to him, "You seem to react to the question of your Jewishness with body, mind and soul." He certainly did!

The experiences of John Knight were typical of the average children of immigrant Jewish parents. Their ghetto world did not exactly fit into a polite Gentile society. As the boy John Knight grew up, he felt a sense of shame that his parents never became Americanized. He felt somewhat inferior over his cultural background and tended to undervalue whatever positive ideals came from his heritage.

At seven he was enrolled in a *Cheder* and required to attend five afternoons a week for an hour or more after the regular public school sessions. The curriculum at the *Cheder* was extremely dull, he relates:

> The studies were completely unrelated to the American scene, and the Hebrew school schedule interfered with the precious hours for daylight games after school. We felt that unfair advantage was being taken of us and rebelled continuously. Our hatred of the *Cheder* was intensified by the method of teaching which was borrowed from the Eastern European Hebrew schools. Out of the anger and frustration of their own lives, the teachers beat the children viciously with very slight provocation, frequently for minor disobedience or errors . . . It was a decidedly painful experience lasting many years.

He found no better pattern of Jewishness in the synagogue. It repelled and terrified him. Contrasted with the churches of the community, it lacked aesthetic appeal and emotional stimulation. John Knight's father, who constantly demanded blind obedience to what appeared to the child as strange customs, refused to discuss the meaning or the necessity of these various rituals. Only unquestioning compliance was the order of the day. Thus, all his formative experiences as a Jew were entwined with taboos and prohibitions. Such was his preparation for adult Jewish living.

It was not surprising that John Knight came to regard his Jewish background as an irritating element in his personality, as something alien and hostile and not intelligible or pleasurable. Never at home in his heritage, how could he ever hope to appreciate its deepest meaning for him?

There is much food for thought in this book. How much of our Jewishness are we still fighting as it once appeared to us in its ancient garments? Today many Jews of all shades of Judaism continue to rebel against *religion* because they still suffer from an anti-authority complex. They are still expressing in their adult life the unsuccessful childhood rebellion that they may have once waged against a dogmatic father or against meaningless ritual or against an uncouth *Melamed*.

The message of John Knight's book is simply this: You can't be happy as a Jew until you stop fighting being a Jew. You must end the vicious cycle of insecurity, anxiety, frustration and rebellion which produced the John Knight's of our time. Instead, you must try to resolve your conflicts about being Jews. And you must make sure that your children find happiness in being Jews.

How then can you be happy as a Jew?

How do you pursue Jewish happiness?

Self-Acceptance

The first link in the chain of Jewish happiness is the word *self-acceptance*. To accept oneself as a Jew means to stop wishing you were something else. That is just what some Jews do. They have "imaginitis." They try to be social climbers among the Blue Book's 400. Maybe you know some Jews like that. I do.

Accepting oneself as a Jew involves renouncing any ideas about being someone else. To be a healthy-minded, real person, self-discovery and self-acceptance are primary. An apple tree does not become more desirable by aspiring to be an oak tree. Just as a tree must first accept its species and then its special habitat in order to bring forth its best fruit, so each of us must accept himself and realize that we are in the situation of the Jews.

Jean Paul Sartre, the French existentialist, recently wrote a brilliant book called *Anti-Semite and Jew*. There he pointed out the Jews have a common bond that transcends religious, cultural, national, or ethnic elements. Jews have one thing in common with each other: *their situation*. They live in a community which takes them for Jews. To be a Jew, Sartre says, is to be thrown into the situation of a Jew. The only question the individual has the freedom to answer is: what kind of a Jew shall he be? Shall he rebel against it, deny it, attempt to escape it? That, says Sartre, is what the "inauthentic Jew" does. Or shall he accept the situation, assume the responsibilities it imposes and live as happily, as gracefully, as meaningfully as he can? That is what the "authentic Jew" does.

The inauthentic Jews are those whom others take for Jews but who have decided to run away from an intolerable situation. They follow the avenue of flight. They have an inferiority complex about being a Jew. They have never accepted themselves as Jews, but instead they accept the propaganda of the anti-Semites who rant and rave that the Jew is something to be abhorred. The inauthentic Jews allow themselves to be poisoned by the contemptuous stereotype that others have of them. They live in fear that their actions, their mannerisms, their names, their noses will correspond to the very stereotype which the anti-Semite labels as "Jewish." They almost become Jewish anti-Semites! And no anti-Semite is quite like the Jewish anti-Semite! So the inauthentic Jews play at not being Jews. The irony is that the inauthentic Jews want to lose themselves in the Christian world and assimilate beyond the shadow of recognition as Jews; yet society forces them to remain fixed in a Jewish milieu, victims of constant tension and overpowering frustration.

Such, for example, were the Jews of nineteenth-century

Germany who tasted the new-found freedom of emancipation and longed to flee from their Jewish past. This they hated. Their answer was flight from Judaism . . . flight to the outside world, to the baptismal font of the church, to any place that would accept them without the label of Jew. They found many doors open to them, but none leading to security or happiness. They were trying too hard for Jewish happiness.

The authentic Jew, on the other hand, accepts himself and ceases pretending what he cannot be. He accepts his situation. He ceases to run away from himself or to be ashamed of his own people. He is the informed Jew. He is the educated Jew. He is the participating Jew.

Sartre thinks that the inauthentic Jew will have more trouble from his Jewishness than the authentic Jew. An authentic Jew, to use Sartre's interesting vocabulary, may suffer minor discomforts over being discriminated against. Maybe he can't get the apartment he wants, or the promotion he seeks, or the accommodations he requests. But the anti-Semite can't touch his integrity. His soul remains undefiled. Hear the sermon of Shakespeare: "To thine own self be true!" Accept yourself! Live with yourself! Be yourself, whatever the cost!

The dilemma in which many modern Jews find themselves is how to be happy with their Jewishness, how to accept themselves and overcome the neurotic feeling of self-hatred that torments their psychic balance.

To pursue Jewish happiness and be happy as Jews, we must feel a genuine sense of loyalty to the Jewish people. Having a sense of belonging will neutralize some of the acids of anxiety and inferiority. After all, you can't run away from yourself. Wherever you go, you take yourself along!

Acceptance of yourself as a Jew involves some difficulties and hardships. Every group finds them. Do you think it is easy for a Negro to be blackfaced? Don't Catholics suffer from bias and prejudice and misunderstanding?

Sometimes I hear a man say to me, "I'm a Jew and I'm proud of it. I never deny I am a Jew. I go to *Shul* on *Yom Kippur* too." He thinks I am impressed. Sorry, but I'm not. He reminds me of Sholom Aleichem's famous characterization of an old Hebrew teacher, blind in one eye, near-sighted in the other. He used to wear spectacles without lenses. Asked why, he would answer triumphantly, "Well, it's better than nothing, isn't it?"

I picture Jews who attend synagogues only on *Yom Kippur* as going, so to speak, to leave their visiting card when calling on the Almighty. It is not as easy as all that. You can't be a happy Jew without pursuing Jewish happiness all year around. It takes time and devotion, it takes self-discovery and self-acceptance, to be a happy kind of authentic Jew.

Part of the secret of happiness is to be satisfied both with what we have and with what we do not have. Some people are not so unhappy with what they have as with what others have. They think that what is far off at a distance is enchanting. Yet the faster they follow after it, the swifter it flies away from them.

So with some Jews. They think being happy is to be like the non-Jews, as un-Jewish as the world will permit. There are too many marginal Jews who are Jews to the Gentiles but not Jews to the Jews. Yet are they happy? They are not satisfied with being de-Judaized. The tinge is still there, like the indelible laundry mark that never fades completely away. Nor are they completely sure they are fully accepted by Gentile society. They think if they can only pursue the Gentile ways faster and harder they will draw closer to Heaven . . . until weary with the chase, they finally discover, at great spiritual cost, that to be happy as a Jew means to accept oneself and to devote oneself to the Jewish people.

No, you can't be happy as a Jew if you are in perpetual protest against being a Jew.

Self-Knowledge

Self-knowledge is therefore the second link in the chain of Jewish happiness. The phrase "know thyself," which comes to us from the ancient Greeks, offers wise insight for modern Jews. Knowledge of oneself, of one's past and one's people . . . knowledge of Judaism.

We Jews have a noble history. From the knowledge of Judaism we have learned that though life can become unbearable with oppression and restriction, we Jews found an inner faith that always sustained our people and enabled them to survive. The annals of our history offer innumerable examples of the victory of the spirit in Judaism. Our people emerged infinitely richer from the bondage of Egypt, from the captivity of Babylon, from the persecutions of Antiochus and Hadrian. The Jew has seen tyrants like the Hitlers and the Stalins of our time come and go. The faith of the Jew in ultimate justice has been confirmed by the transitoriness of dictators in the past. The Jew knows, from the knowledge of his own past, from the history of his experiences, that brutality and injustice cannot last; that the success of totalitarians can be only momentary triumph; that sooner or later, leaders whose power rests on the tyranny of force and the propaganda of hate must succumb to those who champion justice and freedom and brotherhood. We Jews are not afraid of the tomorrow because we have lived through yesterday. That is the faith of self-knowledge.

Self-Appreciation

Self-acceptance and self-knowledge lead inevitably to the third link in the chain—*self-appreciation.* Self-appreciation is not parochial chauvinism, nor inordinate pride, nor overbearing stuffiness, nor conceited arrogance. Self-appreciation as Jews means to appreciate what the Jews have meant to civilization—their contributions to commerce and industry, the arts, sciences and humanities, to philosophy and religion and human thought. Self-appreciation is simply the ability to appreciate your self-worth, to hold your head high and know that you are somebody. It is summed up in two simple words that spell out volumes—*Jewish dignity.*

Just as the synagogues of yesterday were the means of survival, carefully nurturing self-acceptance and self-knowledge and self-appreciation in a time of darkness and persecution, so the synagogues and temples today are dedicated to the same high hope of pressing forward and carrying aloft the dignity of the Jewish faith. The Jew could no more have survived days of old without the encouragement of the synagogue than he could have lived without the nourishment of daily bread. The synagogue gave depth and meaning to his drab existence; it brought comfort and inspiration in times of crisis. The synagogue went with the wandering Jew into every corner of the globe. Its spirit permeated his spirit. Its perpetual light brought hope and purposefulness to his harsh life. There in the sanctity of God's presence the Jew poured out his heart to his partner in the business of life, seeking counsel and wisdom, inspiration and courage from the well-springs of the synagogue. And there he found the strength to carry on. There he found the faith he needed.

Today, in brighter times, our synagogues and temples are seeking to link self-acceptance and self-knowledge with self-appreciation into a chain of strength, so that being a Jew can be a source of joy and happiness . . . so that our youth can like being Jews and our aged not feel cast aside. Our religious schools, housed in beautiful surroundings, taught by trained teachers, using modern progressive educational techniques, are giving our boys and girls a happy Jewish experience. Being a Jew is not linked up with associations in dank, dark vestry rooms, with *Cheder* memories to become nightmares for a John Knight. In our kindergarten, self-acceptance is encouraged through a happy association with things Jewish. Through our social program of temple organizations, every person can find a place for himself, a sense of belonging, and thus opportunity for happy and purposeful fellowship. Through study groups and colleges of Jewish studies and adult classes, through speakers and lecturers and stimulating programs, our people find intellectual satisfactions that make self-knowledge a joyous experience. Through the emotional and spiritual inspiration of worship and prayer, self-acceptance and self-knowledge and self-appreciation become fused into a high entity that links the average Jew with the eternal Jew, a partnership between God and man.

Where else can one find joy in Jewish experience? Need I spell out what the Jewish home has always meant? Must I detail the proud tradition of the Jewish family, the Jewish humor that thrived in the living-room, the ceremonies and observances on the Sabbath or the Seder that clustered around the dining-room table, the delicacies and special dishes that featured the kitchen, the books and magazines, the periodicals and volumes that filled the shelves of the home library . . .

There is joy in Jewish life if you want to seek it. There is Jewish happiness if you choose to pursue it. You can be happy as a Jew if you accept yourself, if you know yourself, if you appreciate yourself.

Let me leave this subject of Jewish happiness by telling you about one who found joy in Judaism and who brought with him a radiance and a glow to Jewish experience that made him immortal. His name was Israel ben Eliezer, but the people chose to call him *Baal Shem Tov,* Master of the Good Name. A strange and wondrous man was he, a kind of true brother to his fellow-man. He was born in the Carpathian Mountains of Southeastern Europe at the beginning of the 18th century. Expelled from *Cheder* at a young age, he took to the mountains, learned the ways of nature—the scents of her herbs and seeds and healing waters. With them he was able to cure certain illnesses and to do wonders that naive people in those days considered miracles. But he was no ordinary faith healer. There was a kindliness, a saintliness that fast won him to the hearts of the ordinary Jewish peasants. They came to him, those tailors and cobblers, teamsters and tavern-keepers, with their sick bodies and sick hearts; and from this Master of the Good Name they learned a simple philosophy for happy living.

God was everywhere and in everything, he said, wherever people went and in whatever they experienced. Life was hard, he admitted, but it need not be sad or mournful. Jewish experience, said the Master of the Good Name, should be gay and joyous. Everyone should wholeheartedly love God and pray to Him, not with tears and terror but with laughter and song, with joy and with enthusiasm. In his simple, gentle way, the Baal Shem Tov taught the Jews of his day to laugh, to sing, and to be happy Jews. He took them out of the shadows that had so long darkened their lives. He brought them back to the sunshine.

In time, the movement he founded (called Hasidism) became abused and distorted, but the spirit of Israel Baal Shem Tov left an imprint in the shifting sands of Jewish history.

There *is* joy in Jewish experience. Go and seek it! There *is* such a thing as Jewish happiness. Pursue it! Then you will discover the secret our generation needs to know —how to be happy as Jews!

PART III

THE RELEVANCE OF REFORM JUDAISM

12. *WHAT IS A REFORM JEW?*

RECENTLY a discussion was reported in a civics class at a Chicago high school that centered around the definition of democracy. The students had been following the news stories on the cold war between East and West. They were mildly interested in fulfilling the assignment, "What is Democracy?". But their replies were stated almost uniformly in the negative: "Democracy is not communist," "Democracy is not totalitarian," "Democracy is not fascist."

The school discussion illustrates an inherent weakness in democracy's propaganda armor. Americans have been accustomed for so long to take for granted their civil rights and their four freedoms that when they are challenged, "What is Democracy? Why is it worth preserving? What does it really stand for?" their replies are too often vague and meaningless. Americans know in a general sort of way that they are against anything communist or fascist, but what they are for remains a greater mystery. One has only to scan the daily headlines to realize how persistently we fail to live up to what we profess. We create our own vulnerability.

Democracy's dilemma finds a striking parallel among Reform Jews. Many of them do not know what they believe. They know what they are not . . . they are *not* orthodox; but what they actually *are* is less clear. For those who do understand the principles of Reform, the gap between what is professed and what is practiced is as wide as democracy's.

History, Ideas, Accomplishments

My first proposition sounds like a self-evident truism, but it isn't quite that simple.

A Reform Jew is one who understands the meaning of Reform Judaism—its history, its ideas, its accomplishments.

Reform Judaism came into being as a movement to save Judaism for the Jew and the Jew for Judaism. During the early years of the nineteenth century, after the spirit of the French Revolution had followed Napoleon's armies through Europe, the ghetto walls were shattered and the restrictions insulating Jews from non-Jewish contacts were lifted. Jews were given the promise of becoming free and equal citizens in the countries where they lived. Education, politics, literature, the arts, were all opened to them. Eagerly, Jews flocked to these new pursuits as moths gather to a bright light. Now to many Jews of the 19th century, freedom from the ghetto meant freedom from Judaism. They felt that as they left the ghetto and became free citizens, they had no further need of Jewish life. The synagogue could be abandoned.

Reform Judaism, having started in Germany as a people's movement, offered a survivalist answer to these false conceptions of emancipation. It sought to modernize the synagogue, to make its public worship and its religious forms up-to-date and acceptable to the modern free spirit of the new Jew. It refined traditional concepts and brought them into harmony with the intellectual standards of the liberal, rational, progressive spirit of the new age. But after a few decades of liberalism, Europe succumbed to reaction. The Jews' emancipation was forfeited. Promised rights were cancelled. Only across the ocean in America did democracy take root, and to America came Jews with liberal ideas. Here in the free soil of this rising frontier state, these ideas took root and found nourishment. For that reason Reform Judaism experienced its greatest development in the United States. It became an American product. It reflected America's liberal spirit.

The basic idea of liberal, progressive Reform Judaism is: Judaism permits change, modification and adjustment to keep up with the contemporary world. Whatever Judaism retains of the past, whether it be ideology or ceremony, must have significance and must have meaning for the present. It must have a relationship to our daily life. Observances must be adjusted to the conditions of modern living. New forms, new concepts must be developed to interpret its spirit for the future.

Such is the essence of Reform's philosophy. The moment Reform Judaism ceases to change and progress, the moment it becomes static and frozen, it ceases to be Reform but something else—just another brand of orthodoxy.

All interpretations of Judaism hold to the fundamental, changeless core of belief in one universal God of goodness who is served by personal and social righteousness, a God of the universe who is the Father of all men, in whose sight all men are brothers. But on the question of Torah, of Revelation—the problem of authority, as it is known in theology—Reform Judaism has departed from older views. This is the key to its door.

Reform accepts the findings of modern Biblical scholarship and holds that the Bible, rather than being the source of all authority . . . "you must do such and such because *Es steht geschrieben*" . . . is instead the source of religious inspiration. The Bible was not written by God for man, as all orthodox religions claim, both Jewish and Christian, but by man about God to help man in his quest for God and his understanding of God. Reform holds that Revelation is not a single event that happened only once on Mount Sinai long ago . . . but God's Revelation is rather a continuous progressive process. God is to be found not only in the Torah but in the wonders of nature, in the processes of human history, in the human intellect and in the individual conscience ages ago and in our own time.

Thus did Reform follow the studies of scientific knowledge brought to light in the past century. Reform Judaism therefore carries with it an intellectual respectability as an adaptable way of thought and life to the cultural and social conditions of the new age.

As a result of the history and ideas of the new interpretation of Judaism, definite accomplishments were achieved which should be understood and appreciated by Reform Jews.

1. Reform has brought Judaism up to date and enabled modern Jews, educated by public and private schools of higher learning, to practice what is no longer a medieval religious relic steeped in superstition.

2. Reform has brought back to Judaism many of our people who had lost interest in the old orthodoxy, who were left unconvinced and uninspired by a religious service which they could barely follow, much less comprehend.

3. By Americanizing historic "old world" practices and by supplying new and inspiring features to Jewish worship, the old synagogue became a modern Temple of God aesthetically beautiful and spiritually uplifting.

4. Reform re-emphasized the importance of Israel's prophetic teachings about social justice and applied them

to contemporary social problems. That is the major emphasis of Jewish preaching today . . . applying prophetic standards to our modern world.

5. And finally, Reform exerted a tremendous influence upon other religious groups within Judaism.

Today, the Conservative movement which started out half a century ago to conserve traditional, orthodox practices has adopted many Reform practices into its synagogues —like confirmation, late Friday evening services, Sunday schools, sisterhoods, youth groups, unions of congregations, even parking lots! Significantly, textbooks and adult educational materials developed by Reform Judaism's Commission on Jewish Education are being widely used by non-Reform congregations, to cite just a few instances of Reform's great influence on the development of American Jewish life.

Clearly the future pattern of Judaism in America is destined to follow the Reform point of view—*if* Reform Jews are made aware of their potential influence for good. A Reform Jew should understand and appreciate something about Reform Judaism . . . the history, the ideas, and the accomplishments of Reform Judaism . . . if he is to be intelligent about his identification.

The Reform Temple

The second broad statement defining what a Reform Jew is follows from the first: *A Reform Jew is one who affiliates himself with an institution of Reform Judaism*— namely a Reform temple.

There are some who think that anyone who isn't orthodox, who doesn't keep a kosher home or pray with covered head must be a Reform Jew. Not at all! Reform is a philosophy of religion, a point of view.

This liberal point of view is embodied in the chief institution of our movement—the Reform temple. Serving as a house of prayer, study and assembly, the Reform temple is the outgrowth of the synagogue of old, *except* that prayers are offered in the vernacular because English is the language of the people. The old prayerbook has been edited and shortened. Men and women sit together as a result of a principle established in Reform that women have equal rights. The Reform temple has introduced into the service magnificent music, employing an organ and choral singing. Dignity and decorum have replaced the old bedlam of coming and going and buzzing conversations on the side. But most important of all, a systematic educational program has been developed, beginning with the consecration of the little ones, culminating with confirmation of 15-year-olds, and continuing on into youth and adult education . . . a system designed to teach young and old the meaning of our faith, the history of our people, the ethics of our tradition, the loyalties that bind all Jews as one religious community brotherhood.

A Jew does not become a Reform Jew by default simply because he isn't orthodox or conservative or reconstructionist. It is not a process of elimination. Only by the active step of identifying himself and his family through membership in a Reform temple does he have the right to call himself a Reform Jew.

Reform Judaism in Private Life

This leads us to a third proposition: *A Reform Jew is one who participates in the program of Reform Judaism in his private life.* There are home ceremonies on various occasions which beautify the home spirit and draw the family closer together . . . on the Sabbath Eve, on Hanukkah with the children, on Passover with the family Seder, on Purim and Succot and the other festivals.

There is much in Reform Judaism which can nourish our withered spiritual growth . . . much that is greatly neglected nowadays. We have gotten away from the emphasis stressed by classical Reform of the importance of home readings and private devotions. The early Reformers were men of learning and culture, at least the leaders of the movement. They insisted that the classics of Jewish literature ought to be translated into English and be made available to the average Jew. Now that work has been done. Today our libraries are full of Jewish literature. There are thousands of volumes on Jewish themes . . . novels, essays, drama, folklore, anthologies, children's stories, nursery tales . . . books for every age level.

Here is doubtlessly where Reform Jews have fallen down the most in recent days. They have relegated the reading of Jewish literature to the Rabbi! And when it comes to the Bible and the Prayerbook, the two great classic source-books of Reform Jewish literature, Reform Jews have fallen down even worse. As Dr. Solomon B. Freehof has noted, there was a time when people read the Bible and the Prayerbook at home. They could quote whole passages. They went over noble thoughts and memorized them and repeated them to their children. Our fathers may have read fewer books, but they read vertically. They read deeply; they pondered the meaning of what they read, and discussed it and reflected on it, and went back and read it again. Nowadays, there seems so little time to read much besides the newspaper, a magazine or two, and maybe the "Book of the Month." We read horizontally, extensively, but without depth or discriminating taste. We read just to keep up on things, if we read at all. A Reform Jew ought to be an informed Jew, not a king-size *am haaretz,* an ignorant Jew.

The purpose of showing the Reform Jew the emotional and intellectual values of his faith is to assist him in fulfilling the prophetic ideals in private life of justice, truth, decency, mercy and love . . . to enable him to carry these over into every day life and make him a better person, a better citizen, a better human being.

"A New Heart and a New Spirit"

The Hebrew word for sin, *chet,* has an interesting etymology. Its root meaning originally was "missing the mark." Sin was a missing of the mark, the way a marksman misses his aim.

It seems to be that many Reform Jews have simply missed the mark. There may be good reasons for that. Many children of an earlier generation have drifted away from Reform at the very time that men and women, once orthodox in their childhood, have drifted toward it. Reform has been woefully at fault in not providing some kind of orientation to its new-found recruits.

When a non-Jewish woman is converted to Judaism, she undergoes an intensive course of study under the personal supervision of the Rabbi, so that she can learn what beliefs, what practices, what obligations she is accepting when she joins the Jewish people. Perhaps some such orientation course ought to be offered to new members of a Reform temple when they first come to Reform Judaism—and periodically to older members who have belonged long enough to forget.

We have been missing the mark. Some of us know what ideas and practices Reform has rejected. Like the supporters of democracy, we know what we are against. But what we are *for,* what we actually *are,* has been less clear. And in a sense one has no right to be *against* something, so long as he is not *for* something. We should "accentuate the positive." Too many are just negative-minded "aginners," as we call them.

Now we understand what a Reform Jew is . . . or should be. A Reform Jew must know the meaning of Reform Judaism . . . its history, its ideas, its accomplishments. He is part of a great movement of the people, affiliated through his membership in a Reform Temple, part of the national Union of American Hebrew Congregations, which binds all congregations in a country-wide group, and maintaining a great Hebrew Union College-Jewish Institute of Religion in Cincinnati, in New York, in Los Angeles, and soon in Jerusalem, to train spiritual leaders who are a credit to their people. He participates in the program of a Reform Temple, unites with others regularly in public worship, in Temple activities, in philanthropies and communal affairs—and carries over its ethics into his private life as an American citizen. He is a better Jew and a better man for having shared the experience of being part of a great religious fellowship. It is not easier or more convenient or less bother to be a Reform Jew—but it is a great experience in Jewish living!

The prophet Ezekiel, who more than any other ancient Jewish theologian framed the Jewish concept of atonement, taught over 2,000 years ago that atonement consists in complete spiritual regeneration, in true penitence and in the amendment of the sinner's way. To his people in his day Ezekiel said: "A new heart also will I give you, and a new spirit will I put within you . . . so that you may walk in My statutes and Mine ordinances and do them . . ." We need a new heart and a new spirit in Reform Jewry today . . . and more heart and more spirit on the part of our people . . . if we are to achieve the spiritual regeneration our age requires for survival.

We are living in a new era of earth satellites and rocket missiles. We cannot run on our reputation or our prestige for long, unless each of us is deeply committed, heart and spirit, to its liberal principles and prepared to carry them forth with enthusiasm and devotion and pride. The challenge now is to go forward in the spirit of our faith and give new meaning, new strength, new heart and new spirit to being an American Reform Jew.

13. *WHY I BELIEVE IN REFORM JUDAISM*

Let us begin and approach this chapter from two standpoints. First, what Reform Judaism will not stand for, and secondly, the positive, what it does stand for.

What Won't Reform Judaism Stand For?

What won't Reform Judaism stand for? First, Reform Judaism will not stand for a *secular* interpretation of Jewish life. Reform believes that our religion is the reason for our existence—not anti-Semitism, not philanthropy, not charity, not the super-abundance of various secular organizations which dot the scene of the American Jewish community. Most of these organizations and causes are worthy in themselves, but unfortunately, too many Jews in America make one or more of these their religion instead of subsuming the cause as one aspect of our religion, Judaism. Some people have the naive notion that merely by writing out a check to the United Jewish Appeal they are good Jews, or that joining the B'nai B'rith or the Anti-Defamation League is enough automatically to make them Jews in good standing.

Nor will Reform stand for the *nationalist* interpretation of Jewish life, which makes Zionism or Israel the sole reason and exclusive purpose for Jewish survival. Now the cause of Israel has its rightful place in Jewish life and is supported proudly and generously by Reform Jewish leaders. But neither Zionism nor the cause of Israel can take the place of our religion.

Reform Judaism will not stand for the *escapist interpretation of assimilation.* Alas, there are too many Jews who feel they are born a Jew and can do nothing more about it. They may go with Jews socially, and say "some of my best friends are Jews," but they remain indifferent, unidentified, unaffiliated, untutored, illiterate about things Jewish. Such Jews worship the altars of the three monkeys: they hear no Judaism, they feel no Judaism, they practice no Judaism. They do not realize that one becomes a Jew by the actions of others—one's parents—but one remains a Jew by his own actions.

Still another false interpretation of Jewish life that Reform Judaism will not stand for is the *ancestor worship idea.* We have too many Reform Jews who in days gone by used to carry the attitude of the Boston Brahmins. They refused to rub shoulders with those whom they felt were "untouchables." Some Reform Jews used to boast about where their grandfathers came from, as if in some mysterious fashion this prevented them from mixing or mingling with any other Jews. Back in the mid-nineteenth century, Reform Judaism was identified almost solely with German Jews. But this is no longer true. Reform Judaism happily belongs to all Jews in America, whether their origins be German or East European or Sephardic, regardless of where their fathers and grandfathers came from. Reform Judaism will not stand for the kind of religious snobbishness or false pride that engendered so much ill-will of our fellow Jews a generation or two ago.

Nor will Reform Judaism stand for the *superstitious interpretation of Jewish life,* for the old wives' tales and the irrelevant folklore that interlarded many ceremonies and customs hoary with age, whose significance has long since been outlived and discarded by Reform. Ceremonies like *chalitzah* (release from Levirate marriage), the *Get* (divorce decree), auctioning the *mitzvot* (fund-raising in the synagogue service prior to reading the Torah), the role of the *agunah* (a woman legally barred from remarriage), *pidyon habben* (redemption of the first born), wearing of the tefillin (prayer phyllacteries), or such orientalisms as wearing a hat at worship, taking off one's shoes on the pulpit, or facing only east when praying—these are customs which may once have had meaning to Jews, but which have today lost their relevance to modern American Jews.

There are other negative aspects of Jewish life that Reform Judaism will not stand for, but you cannot define a dynamic faith in terms of the negative. Let us "accentuate the positive." What is it that Reform Judaism stands for that makes me and so many, many others believe in it with all our hearts and souls and might?

The Idea of Change

The idea of change is basic to what Reform Judaism stands for. Reform asserts that it has the right to make changes in religious practices, to adapt older practices and customs to newer days, to discard what is no longer useful, to create new ceremonies that will meet the religious requirements of the new generation. Indeed, every generation has the right and the responsibility to make changes that seem necessary in the outward observances of Judaism.

Rabbi Joseph Klein writes a trenchant critique on this point: [1]

"Reform" means to remake or change for the better. A person who reforms is one who changes his habits or way of life so that he becomes a better individual. A government may find that certain of its old laws make it possible for many evils to occur in Government, and it will therefore institute reforms, meaning that the old laws are repealed and new laws adopted so that the evils are prevented and better government results. Similarly, a religious movement may find that some of its ideas and beliefs are no longer accepted by its followers; or that certain of its traditions and customs have become outmoded and meaningless with the passage of time. Reforms then become necessary and they may consist of eliminating certain ideas and customs or creating new modes of religious expression. Often the reform may consist of going back to an old idea or way of belief that had been in force in the far distant past, but which had become so overgrown with cumbersome detail that the original idea was no longer recognizable. Just as a tree must sometimes be pruned of its dead branches, if it is to be healthy and bear fruit, so it is necessary sometimes to cut out the dead branches of meaningless prayers, rituals, customs, and beliefs from a religious movement, if the religion is to be a healthy one and serve its followers in a healthy way.

Modern Reform Judaism has no intention of denuding Jewish life of its vitality or of casting out old forms merely for the sake of casting them out. On the contrary, it seeks to revitalize the spiritual heritage of the past by giving a stronger emphasis to that which is primary and fundamental in Judaism by eliminating the unnecessary and cumbersome dead branches of centuries. Its goal is to create a dynamic and wholesome faith of the 20th century for 20th-century Jews. It welcomes both old and new ideas and forms if they are of the kind that quicken the Jew to spiritual reawakening. It recognizes that change is wholesome and good, for change means growth and progress. It sifts and measures and seeks the best that the Jewish past has to offer, and rejects that which is of little value for today or tomorrow. Above all, it searches constantly, as did its prophetic forbears of ancient time, for truth concerning God and man, for the best way in which a man can serve his fellow man and his God.

[1] Temple Bulletin, Worcester, Mass., April 7, 1954.

The Religious Interpretation of Jewish Survival

In the light of this idea of change which is so fundamental to the religious philosophy of Reform Judaism, it is obvious that Reform Judaism stands for the religious interpretation of Jewish survival. We are Jews primarily by reason of our religion and our religious identification. It is for this that we have survived the tyranny of the majority. It is by this that we have survived as a unique people through all the weary centuries.

Because Reform Judaism believes in the religious interpretation of Jewish survival, we have developed definite affirmations and convictions about the belief in God, the problem of revelation, the function and efficacy of prayer, belief in immortality of the soul, the nature of man, the mission of Israel, and other important theological convictions central to the religious interpretation of Judaism. This is what Reform Judaism stands for.

Since religion is central in the constellation of Jewish values for Reform Judaism, we Reform Jews have taken justifiable pride in the dignity and decorum of our worship. We have found it necessary to modify certain rituals in order to make worship more meaningful, to change or reform certain prayers in order to make them more understandable, and more a reflection of the spiritual aspirations of the modern Jew. As a result we have developed the Union Prayerbook which is used in over 550 Reform temples throughout the country. Most prayers are offered in English, not because Reform Judaism opposes Hebrew (as some mistakenly believe) but because prayer must be understood by both the heart and the mind. Unfortunately the realities of Jewish life in America are such that most of our people regrettably do not understand Hebrew. It is more important that they understand the prayers they offer with a sincere heart, even though such prayers be in the language of the people, than to parrot mechanically and without comprehension in the *Lashon Kadosh,* the sacred tongue of Hebrew. Indeed, even the Talmud justifies this procedure of offering prayers in the vernacular so that people can understand what they are praying. Reform Judaism affirms that services of worship must be intelligent, rational, and intellectually respectable, for sincere prayer in any language is holy.

A Liberal View on Scriptures

In the third place, Reform Judaism stands for a *liberal interpretation of Scriptures.* This is a fundamental distinction between Orthodoxy and Reform. Orthodoxy insists that the Scriptures were literally written by God for man, and therefore every one of the 613 positive and negative commandments of the Torah must be literally fulfilled. Reform Judaism, on the other hand, following the scientific scholarship of the school of higher criticism, affirms that the Bible is written by man about God, written by inspired men seeking the meaning of God and the essence of God. Consequently, the Bible is not to be obeyed simply because of fundamentalist theology or immovable tradition, but rather because it inspires us with its eternal truths and prophetic spirit and ethical insights.

This understanding of the Bible undergirds the attitude of Reform Judaism toward rituals and ceremonies. These in themselves are not sacred cows. Ceremonials and rituals are observed because they are meaningful, because they are symbols of ethical or moral principles. The prophets of ancient Israel—Amos, Hosea, Isaiah, Jeremiah—taught that when the ceremony becomes more important than the ethical principle, Judaism is dead. Reform Judaism underscores prophetic Judaism.

Thus, Reform Judaism stands for the idea that any custom or ceremony or ritual must be meaningful and significant to the individual. As a result, many customs and rituals have been dropped or abandoned and still others have been reintroduced.

For example, the second-day observance of Jewish holidays has been discarded by Reform Judaism because the original reason for instituting a second day of observance has long since disappeared, namely the uncertainty of the Jewish calendar, and the necessity of notification by means of runners and bonfires on the Palestinian hilltops announcing a new moon, or new holiday or festival.

Or another example: prayers in the traditional prayerbook about the sacrificial system have been discarded and removed because the ancient temple in Jerusalem no longer exists.

Or consider the laws of Kashruth and kosher foods: Reform Judaism considers their observance no longer essential to being a good Jew because the original purpose of the laws of Kashruth, namely, to keep Jews distinctive, separate and apart from non-Jews by means of forbidden foods, is no longer valid in modern life; nor has the sanitary aspect of the laws of Kashruth become necessary nowadays with all the scientific paraphernalia for cleanliness and refrigeration which the meat and packing industries have developed in modern times.

The right to abrogate also implies the right to introduce. The important point of ceremonies and rituals, not always understood, is that Reform Judaism stands for the right to introduce new ceremonies and new customs that are not traditional in themselves, but which have great meaning. For example, late Friday evening services were instituted, or in some cases Sunday morning services, for the same reason: to give our people an opportunity of coming to worship at a time when they were not working. Late Friday evenings as a time for Sabbath services in Reform temples have become traditional for two generations, but it is pertinent to point out that this innovation is not traditional nor is the time sacrosanct. As a matter of fact, some people in the Reform Jewish movement have predicted that with the coming of the five-day week, and Saturday again a day of rest, a day away from one's office or factory or job, the Saturday morning service may some day once again become the principal service.

To take another example of a new ceremony introduced by Reform Judaism: Confirmation is only a little over a hundred years old, but it has become so meaningful and has become associated with so many beautiful memories that it has grown into one of the high points in the religious calendar of Reform Judaism. The same goes for the ceremony of consecration introduced in the 1930's, when little children entering the Religious School for the first time are blessed by the rabbi.

The point is that Reform Judaism stands for the principle of observing customs and ceremonies and ritual only when they are significant and meaningful—not just mechanical or automatic observance. Ceremonies are important educational devices, but only when they are sincere and inspiring symbols for teaching of deeper, ethical or moral principles.

The Intellectual Basis of Religion

The fourth idea Reform Judaism stands for is the *intellectual basis of religion.* Judah Leon Magnus, for many years President of the Hebrew University on Mount Scopus in Jerusalem, taught that the secret of Jewish survival all through the centuries was learning. Indeed, the Jewish concept of "Torah" places a high emphasis on knowledge and learning and study as precious values of our religion.

Reform Judaism has taken seriously the obligation for learning and developed an elaborate educational system which has established through our religious schools a systematic and orderly arrangement of religious instruction in the history, belief, practices, rituals, problems of Reform Judaism.

We have built imposing, well-organized, religious schools and created materials, textbooks, teaching aids, professional standards. We have developed an educational system with a strong retentive power encouraging children to remain within the school for eight years and longer. In addition, Reform Judaism has developed a youth program designed to meet the intellectual, social, educational and spiritual needs of our teen-agers, and thus strengthen their attachments to Judaism and the Jewish institutions at this impressionable age. In recent years, Reform Judaism has also instituted an educational program for adults, and while this is just in the beginning stages, it has already made significant inroads with the establishment of study groups, seminars, round tables, colleges of Jewish studies, and the like, for the intellectual and educational advancement of our people.

The Role of the Individual

Reform Judaism stands for the active participation of the individual. Reform temples are not only imposing houses of worship, but houses of study and houses of assembly as well, with activities for everyone, with active organizations developed like sisterhoods, men's clubs, youth groups, young marrieds and so forth. All this gives an opportunity to every member of the family for personal involvement and personal participation.

Indeed, Reform Judaism needs this personal sense of commitment more than ever. It is not enough to just pay dues. A man does not belong to a cause or to a movement simply with a checkbook and a stroke of a pen. The fate of Reform Judaism's whole future lies in the responsibility of the individual person who identifies himself not only with his temple and with Reform Judaism, but with the Jewish people as well. This sense of identification with the Jewish people gives Reform Jews a sense of belonging. It links us with our brethren everywhere, whether we live in Detroit, New York, Rome, Tel Aviv or Bombay. The personal identification of each Reform Jew through his Temple with the Jewish people everywhere achieves this sense of continuity that stretches back in unbroken succession to the days of the prophets and the sages and the Pharisees and the Rabbis.

These, then, are some of the things that Reform Judaism stands for. These are also some of the things that Reform Judaism does not stand for. But above all, the love of learning, the love of the Jewish people, the love of God, the love of faith, remind us that Reform Judaism is fulfilling the statement ascribed to the Zohar, that "God, Torah and Israel are One." This is religion in action.

14. *REFORM JUDAISM AND THE PROPHETIC IDEAL*

A century and more ago when the leaders of the Reform Jewish movement were casting about for authority to buttress their liberal views of universalism, they turned to the ancient prophets of Israel and found a renewal of inspiration. As the early Reformers denied the legalism and the binding authority of the Halacha and the various rabbinic codes, they latched onto the prophetic concept of liberalism, embracing all humanity. This seemed the appropriate undergirding framework for those starry-eyed 19th-century idealists, for universalism's concern for all mankind, regardless of national boundaries or class distinctions, represented the prophets at their best. Indeed, if you take away the prophetic concept of universalism, Liberal Judaism is stripped naked. The prophetic ideal revolves as the very core of the Reform ideal.

No more fascinating group of men in all literature exists than those giants of the spirit, the prophets. They have never ceased to stir our imagination by the imagery of their words or the power of their personality. They were brave men—fearless, patriotic, public-spirited, men who were overwhelmed by an irresistible compulsion to speak out the truth they felt in their hearts. They were not academic philosophers; they were not ivory-towered theologians. They were simple men of the people who felt God in their hearts, stirred to denounce the wrong-doing they beheld in the social order. Their single purpose was to shape the national, social, and political life of their world in accordance with God's ways. Preservers of piety, voices of Israel's conscience, they were public servants *par excellence,* regardless of personal suffering or sacrifice.

We can learn much from the prophetic ideal to make us better Jews. Consider these three points: 1) their concept of the reality of God; 2) their insistence on righteous living as a corollary of ethical monotheism, and 3) their plea for pure religion, simplicity in religion, rather than excessive ritual or ceremonial trappings. If we understand these three basic ideas, we will be not only better Jews, but better human beings.

The religion of the Hebrew prophets is not as simple to formulate as one might think. The prophets, after all, offered no one single system of thought. Theirs was not one group or school of philosophy. Indeed, the prophets often disagreed with each other as they emphasized different aspects of life. Professor Sheldon H. Blank aptly points out that when we speak of the religion of the Hebrew prophets, we mean "some of the things that some of them said." The earnestness of the prophets bordered on fanaticism, for the prophets were fanatics, ready to sacrifice themselves to martyrdom. They did not hesitate to be troublemakers or disturbers of the peace. Amos had to be deported; Jeremiah was jailed. These were men of wild mien and manner who taught ideas shocking to their contemporaries. The authorities often considered them dangerous and sought to silence them.

The prophets were bold enough to ask, "What in religion is really essential? What does God really want?" Bear in mind that the role of the prophets, as Professor Blank says, was to seek in "mind and deed to improve human society and to promote the brotherhood of man." Their role was not to console or comfort, though some of them did this at certain times in their ministries. The prophets did not primarily create a warm sense of confidence and well-being. Essential to their role was "to make men uneasy and uncomfortably conscious of their obligations."

How did they carry out this role? The prophets were supreme patriots, but their patriotism was of a special sort. What mattered to them was not the wealth or the power of the state, but its spiritual and moral worth. "The prophets believed," writes H. H. Rowley in *The Relevance of the Bible,* "that the power of God was great enough to rescue Israel from the hands of its oppressors, if only Israel would cultivate in its life those qualities which were dearest to the heart of God Himself. This was an altogether deeper patriotism—the desire to see their country not so much great, as good, and the conviction that unless it were good, it could not become truly great."

This is the same idea that Carl Schurz had when he improved on Stephen Decatur's famous statement, "My country right or wrong; when right to be kept right, when wrong to be made right."

Let us consider, then, those three prophetic ideals that changed the course of Judaism, and indeed of the world, which are relevant to Reform Judaism today and its commitment tomorrow.

The Reality of God

The first of the great prophetic ideals that laid the foundations of the religion of the Hebrew prophets was the concept of the reality of God. The reality of God is the basis of their preaching. The prophet Jeremiah summed it up in these words: [1]

> Thus saith the Lord:
> Let not the wise man glory in his wisdom,
> Neither let the mighty man glory in his might,
> Let not the rich man glory in his riches;
> But let him that glorieth, glory in this,
> That he understandeth and knoweth Me,
> That I am the Lord who exercise mercy,
> Justice, and righteousness, in the earth;
> For in these things I delight,
> Saith the Lord.

The prophets believed that God was indwelling in every person, present in man, what the theologians called immanence, and the prophets therefore preached that by heeding God's presence, man can feel the presence of God and promote His divine purposes. The unknown prophet of the exile, Deutero-Isaiah, expressed it in Isaiah 57:15:

> For thus saith the High and Lofty One
> That inhabiteth eternity, whose name is Holy:
> I dwell in the high and holy place,
> With him also that is of a contrite and humble spirit,
> To revive the spirit of the humble,
> And to revive the heart of the contrite ones.

The late Professor Moses Buttenwiser of the Hebrew Union College, whose writings in biblical research contributed much insight, wisely pointed out that the prophetic idea of God being present in every human heart was one idea which changed the thinking of the world. No longer was there any occasion for the indirect method of approach between God and man. Communion with God was to be attained not by mystic rights or priestly mediation, but by personally living up to the Divine

[1] Jeremiah 9:22–23.

promptings within oneself, aspiring at a life of harmony with God, the absolute perfection; in a word, by *righteous, moral living*. Thus, righteousness was realized to be the bond which can bring man closer to God, and morality, henceforth, became the object and the end of religion. *Moral perfection became the prophetic ideal.*

This sounds self-evident to us, but remember this was a revolutionary idea that the prophets contributed to religious thought. Righteous living meant to the prophets: First, whatever God is, we must be like Him. If He is righteous, we must be righteous; if He is holy, we must be holy too; if He is gracious, then we must be gracious. If we truly reverence a God of this character, then we must build up in our lives those rich, ethical qualities which belong to the essence of God. Second, unless we do, thus, strive to become as Godlike as humanly possible, we do not truly worship Him. All our outward forms of worship are an offense to Him, unless behind the form is the substance of the prophetic idea—the reality of God.

Ethical Monotheism

The insistence of the prophets upon the reality of God led them to the doctrine of ethical monotheism and its requirement of righteous living, which is the second of the prophetic ideals. "What doth the Lord require of thee?" asked Micah. "Only to do justice, to love mercy, and to walk humbly with thy God."

The prophetic ideal taught our people that to do the will of God means to make human life better. The test of a man's religion was the way in which he acted. No hypocrisy or insincerity could be allowed. Religion became not only what you say to God, but what you do to man, for as the prophet Habakkub taught, "The righteous man liveth by his faith." The prophetic ideal, therefore, led to the practice of the good life. *Belief had to be buttressed by right living.*

This conviction made the prophets carping critics of the social order. They raised their voices in protest against injustice and oppression. They believed that the work of religion is to help create a world where no one is oppressed. They were determined to make the world a good place to live in. Politics on this basis was everyone's plain religious duty. So, too, was economics. Problems of wealth and poverty were keenly analyzed in the prophetic writings. Amos became the ancestor of all labor agitators. His book was the first recorded attack of labor upon capital. The prophets never enunciated a creed or stated a dogma or essayed a definition of anything they believed. They were not theologians. *The only test of a man's religion to which they gave a thought was the way that a man acted.*

The religion of the prophets was directed toward bringing about a good life for man. The prophets rejected ritual because far from being a help it was often an obstacle. Its tendency was always to become an easy substitute. They never said, "Believe this and you shall live," or "Do this and that and be saved."

The greatness of the prophets consisted in their conception of what God's will was. They had a vision of what was possible for man, a vision at no time even approximately realized in the nearly three thousand years between them and us, yet so important to human life that it has never been dismissed. It has never been put in the category of the dream palaces men are always building to console themselves for things as they are . . . no sky pilots who build "castles in the air," or for "pie in the sky by and by." As Edith Hamilton puts it in her book *Spokesmen for God,* "The prophets saw a world where no man was wronged by another, where the strong shared with the weak, where no individual would be sacrificed for an end as a means to an end, where each individual was prepared to sacrifice something of himself for the end of making what God wished would become a realized good. The prophets showed us what we know should be."

The prophetic ideal, therefore, was to encourage men to work and to create a world where no one would be oppressed. The prophets were not interested in their own salvation. They kept their feet always on the ground, their eyes always on human life, their interest directed only to improve it, never upon themselves.

The prophetic ideal of ethical monotheism, of social justice based upon the doctrine of ethical monotheism, has a ringing message for Reform Jews of today, indeed for all mankind. Have you ever stopped to consider what the prophets would say if they were alive today? What message they would bring on troublesome questions, such as desegregation, race relations, capital and labor, disarmament, world peace? What do you think they would say about our standards and values and our way of thinking? What do you think the prophets would say if they were alive today to a nation that is absorbed in seeking its own pleasures, that has replaced reverence for life with gross materialism, a nation that has enthroned the dollar sign as king and the stock exchange as the holy of holies, whose desire to escape the responsibilities of citizenship is overpowered only by its desire to find a listless, passive peace of mind of the drug addict. Why, the prophets would preach at the top of their voices that such a nation is headed for disaster! A nation that has been drugged by comfort, pleasure, luxury, high-living, Hollywood, the comics; a nation where millions of black-skinned and brown-skinned peoples are exploited by greedy, gouging whites; a nation whose people are cheated of their dignity as human beings because they earn their living by the sweat of their brow—such a nation is headed for disaster!

Shakespeare said it about a Jew; the prophets could have said it about labor. "Hath not a worker eyes, hands, organs, dimensions, affections, passions . . . fed with the same food, hurt with the same weapons, subject to the same diseases, healed by the same means, warmed and cooled by the same winter and summer . . . if you prick him does he not bleed? . . . if you wrong him shall he not revenge?" If the prophets were alive today, if Amos were to speak at Times Square as he did at Beth El of old, he would denounce the discrimination and callousness, the abuse of power and the worship of mammon that undermines the security of this country.

If Isaiah could speak today, he would point not to the hosts of Assyria threatening the inner security of the nation, but to the leeches of communism feeding upon a sick democracy in punishment for having failed to live up to its preachments, a democracy that fails to meet the two greatest problems of our time—*poverty* and *color;* a democracy that steadily refuses to keep faith with its founders, for those who have lived and died for its liberal principles. The prophets, with their faith in the Divine providence, in the Master of the Universe who uses nations and peoples as tools of his master plan of history, would go about the country pointing out how the class conflict of communism feeds on just such situations of injustice that western democracy has created. They would predict doom and disaster to the people unless they mended their ways . . . unless they looked carefully to their civil rights . . . unless they guaranteed greater educational opportunities without quotas and more equitable economic security . . . unless the people found a new sense of justice that would be "of the people, by the people, for the people," not just for the rich, for the Republicans, for the whites, or for the Christians, but for all the children of God.

If the prophets were alive today, they would roam the streets and boulevards of our land. They would also go back of the yards, to the slums and festering blighted areas of squalor and misery. They would ride the Jim Crow buses of the South, visit the "separate but never equal" schools of Mississippi, and the disgrace of America would explode in their souls. They would cry out in the market place, anger some, annoy some, win some, but cause all to think. Their lips, like Isaiah's, would become burning coals with their insistence that brotherhood, like freedom, is indivisible. It is for all or for none. It is not the color of one's skin, or the contour of one's head, but the warmth of one's heart, the skill of one's hands, the fervor of one's soul, that is precious in the sight of God and should be precious in the sight of man. The words of Amos would blaze forth once again. "Are ye not as the Ethiopians unto me, O Children of Israel?"

And the prophets would today summon up the ancient Talmudic story. In the beginning, God created one man and one woman. For this creation, God took dust from the four corners of the earth, so that in later years, even in 20th-century America, no human being could ever boast that his ancestry was superior to that of another, but instead all would realize that they stem from a common fraternity that makes us all brothers under the skin. "Have we not all one Father, hath not One God created us all; why, then, do we deal treacherously one man with his brother?" The prophet's name was Malachi, prophet of universal brotherhood.

If the prophets were alive today, they would follow the reporters of the *New York Times* who recently did such a brilliant survey of the social revolution now confronting the South on ending racial segregation in the schools. The prophets would awaken the slumbering conscience of the South, denounce the timidity and the resistance and the subterfuge circumventing the Supreme Court's decision. The prophets would stand on the steps where the White Citizens' Councils are meeting and rail against the open defiance of these white supremacy groups —shades of the Ku Klux Klan! They would denounce the color blindness of what should be education's only target —ignorance. The prophets would not permit the Supreme Court's mandate to proceed with "deliberate speed" to mean absolute stoppage. They would shout aloud that moderation is not a moratorium on progress. The prophets would throw a searchlight on the anxieties and taboo-like fears that cluster around segregation, both in the South and the North, and on the demagogues who deliberately exploit these anxieties and fears for their own political or economic advantage. If the prophets were alive today, they would be the first to point out that desegregation is not merely a political issue; it involves fundamental human dignity. It is a religious problem. It is a moral issue about which the principles of Judaism must be clear-cut.

The prophetic ideal is as clear as the words of Rabbi Maurice N. Eisendrath, when he spoke at the Paris meeting of the World Union of Progressive Judaism Conference in 1955: "Because of the demands of our own Hebraic teachings, we Jews must stand in the van of those who would rid our respective nations in the world of every semblance of bigotry and prejudice—man against his brother man."

The prophetic ideal, championing the cause of social

justice and social action, has a very relevant message to the Reform Jews of our time. Those lonely, solitary prophets who spoke for God were interested not in advancing any one economic formula over another, but in championing the cause of social justice. They attacked vehemently and bitterly those who abused the responsibilities of wealth and power through their greed and exploitation. Their one force was the will of God speaking out for justice, mercy and holiness in the lives of men and nations. The point to note, as Rabbi Beryl Cohon points out in his splendid book on *The Prophets,* is that "the prophets did not seek to bring justice into a world by merely reorganizing the external forms of society. They sought a transformation of the inner man into a nobler man, a more just world, a new heart and a new mind, mankind speaking a purer tongue—these would come if the will of God prevailed in the lives of men and nations." Both the strength and the weakness of the prophets lie in the fact that they did not implement their ideas. Their visions of justice, mercy and holiness are eternal. The prophetic ideals are always eternal.

My revered teacher, the late Professor Samuel S. Cohon once told his students at the Hebrew Union College that the genius of the prophets in the realm of religion was to be "the lightning rods, which are first struck by the fire of God. Their minds are sensitized to receive the impressions of Divine justice, love and holiness." The prophets, therefore, made their profound contribution to the moral life of mankind by thus serving as his lightning rods, bringing the fire of God down to earth. The ideals they gave mankind made the prophets immortal.

To carry on the unfinished tasks of prophetic religion, to translate these ancient but eternal ideas into contemporary society, to apply eternal truths to ephemeral events

—this is the unending function of modern Judaism in doing the will of God. That is why it is worthwhile to understand and appreciate the ideas that the prophets taught, for they built the foundations of all western religions, especially our own Judaism. They were mankind's first and foremost spokesmen for God.

For Reform Jews today, then, the prophetic ideal urges them to carry forward their message into social action. That is why hundreds of Reform congregations all over the United States have established Social Action Committees to bring the prophetic message into community affairs. This is the moral mandate of Judaism: to carry the prophetic ideal of social justice into the market place and mill and mine, to the farm and factory and forum—to "do justly" and cause the work of righteousness to become peace.

The Place of Rituals

The third great prophetic ideal besides the reality of God and the requirement of righteous living was the plea of the prophets for simplicity in religion, for pure religion. The prophets went into the desert to commune with God. They were simple, God-intoxicated men. The sight of the people of Israel becoming cosmopolitan and sophisticated, waxing rich at the expense of the poor whom they trampled under foot, engaged in aping foreign ways and cultures, aroused the prophets to preach the way of return. They called out to the ancient people of Israel, "Return unto the Lord thy God."

It might be well if Reform Jews caught up in a frenzy of materialistic values, worshipping the gods of Mammon and Success, were to be cautioned, "This is not the way. Return unto the Lord thy God."

The prophets taught pure religion—the dependence of the individual not upon power or glory or material things, but upon God. The prophets inveighed heavily against the abuses of the sacrificial cult, against ceremonial worship as a substitute for spirituality and ethical behavior. Today's preoccupation with reliance on ritualism often takes men's minds away from central matters of religion. When excessive concern over ceremonialism diverts people's minds from the spiritual inwardness of religion, then must we become suspicious of man-made material aids for approaching God. Righteousness must not be usurped by ritual.

Did the prophets oppose ritual itself? No, not completely. Ritual has value only "when it was the organ of the worship of the Lord, and not when it was the substitute for that worship." When God was outwardly honored with a stately ritual by men who rejected from their hearts all those high qualities which inhere in God Himself, their ritual was an offense to Him and a fundamental dishonor to His Name, since it was merely a hollow pretense. Jeremiah pleaded for obedience to the will of God—for an immediate and intimate fellowship with God. "I will put My law in their inward parts, and in their heart will I write it; and I will be their God, and they shall be My people; and they shall teach no more every man his neighbour, and every man his brother, saying: 'Know the Lord'; for they shall all know Me, from the least of them unto the greatest of them, saith the Lord." [1]

The religion of the Hebrew prophets, then, was not any *quid pro quo,* whereby worshipers would bring something to the Deity and ask in return for some favor or re-

[1] Jeremiah 31:33–34.

ward. The unknown prophet of the exile, Deutero-Isaiah, held up for scorn "Yom Kippur Jews." Ever since his time, his words have been read as the Haftarah portion on Yom Kippur:

> Is this the fast that I have chosen?
> The day for a man to afflict his soul?
> Is it to bow down his head as a bulrush,
> And to spread sackcloth and ashes under him?
> Wilt thou call this a fast,
> And an acceptable day to the Lord?
> Is not this the fast that I have chosen?
> To loose the fetters of wickedness,
> To undo the bands of the yoke,
> And to let the oppressed go free,
> And that ye break every yoke?
> Is it not to deal thy bread to the hungry,
> And that thou bring the poor that are cast out to thy house?
> When thou seest the naked, that thou cover him? [1]

To worship God, therefore, was to do what God commanded, and his commandment was to bring justice and mercy. His worship had no connection whatever with anything done in a temple. It had to do entirely with the heart, with man's action toward each other. There was no conceivable form of worship which would bring man in relation with Him. The only way to find Him was to do His will.

To Reform Judaism today, the present rash of ritualism that has broken out in many congregations should be regarded as a symptom of spiritual sickness. Reform Jews observe meaningful ceremonials, not because they are God-given (as orthodox Jews believe), but because they are man-created to make us feel closer to God, closer to our Jewishness. They give emotional and aesthetic warmth, uniting us with *K'lal Yisrael.* But when ritual coagulates into a code and is hailed as a sure-cure nostrum for healing all

[1] Isaiah 58:2–6.

our congregational ailments, when Reform congregations jump on the bandwagon of the religious revival going on in mid-twentieth century America and exploit ritual as a means of enticing confused, once-orthodox Jews into a temple, then it is time to remember the prophetic ideal, and realize that rituals by themselves, no matter how attractively packaged in a code, cannot be a smoke screen to hide a spiritual vacuum. Judaism will not be saved by gimmicks. Rituals are what we live *with,* not what we live *by*. There is a famine in the land, said the ancient prophet Amos, "not a famine for bread nor a thirst for water, but of hearing the word of God."

Spokesmen for God

The prophets were spokesmen for God, the God of all humanity, indeed of all groups. They communed with God in the silence of the night. They were haunted by a vision. As true prophets, they were set apart from their fellow-man. They were in the busy places of the world—in the market places of the city, gates of the Temple, and even in the palace, but always they were lonely individuals. We know little of their lives. Amos was a solitary figure, tending his sheep and caring for his sycamores in the land described in the Bible as a waste and howling wilderness. Hosea's family life and his marriage were tragic. Isaiah, though associating with royalty, kept his own counsel. Jeremiah never married. Ezekiel might have been surrounded by many people, but he shared in all the sorrows of those who were in a strange land. As for the Second Isaiah, the unknown prophet of the Exile, we know nothing—not even his name.

The prophets were solitary, lonely figures, but they were spokesmen for the God of all creation. It was one of the main ideas running through their teachings, the keynote of their preaching, that God is the Father of all men and that all men are His children. They are, therefore, to treat each other as members of one human family. Their continuous plea was for people to practice in their dealings with each other what David Goldberg calls "the seven virtues or graces of justice, righteousness, compassion, mercy, lovingkindness, truth and humility." If people did that, they would be doing God's will.

For the prophetic ideal, men have been forever searching, and for the prophetic ideal they are searching still to this very day.

15. *THE STATE OF ISRAEL AND THE REFORM JEW*

There is a good bit of history behind the question of Israel and the Reform Jew. Classical Reform Judaism of the nineteenth and early twentieth century maintained that Judaism was only a religion and had nothing to do with the political aspirations of Jewish nationalism. The first two generations of Reform rabbis were products of their times. They were strongly anti-Zionist and felt that Zionism was out of keeping with the spirit of early Reform Judaism. And so it was. Again and again, as the issue came before the conventions of the Central Conference of American Rabbis, the Reform rabbis vigorously opposed the movement that would create a Jewish state in Palestine.

How Reform Judaism Changed Its Attitude

In a sense, one man changed the thinking of a generation: Adolf Hitler. His atrocities against the Jews, his diabolical fanaticism that ended in the butchering of six million of our people, created catastrophic needs of those who survived the slaughter. They had to leave Europe. Where were they to go? One country after another, including our own beloved America, denied sanctuary to the Jews. A state of their own became a humanitarian necessity. Postponed by World War II, its establishment became the United Nation's first order of business, its first test case. In 1948, the State of Israel became a reality. Today almost two million Jews, wanderers from the four corners of the earth, dwell in a state that says to them, "You are at home!"

Still, the establishment of a Jewish commonwealth in 1948 was a complete reversal of 1,878 years of Jewish life. Not since the destruction of the second Temple in Jerusalem, in the year 70 of the common era, had Jews dwelt in a homeland of their own. During all that period of time, Jews had lived in the various countries of the world, at times as citizens, at times disenfranchised and dispossessed of even elementary human rights. The French Revolution saw the dawn of a new day, a vision of liberty, equality, fraternity for all—even for Jews. But the spirit of the French Revolution was short-lived. With the post-Napoleonic period came reaction, oppression, degradation, disenfranchisement. More disappointment, more frustration came in the abortive revolution of 1848. In the 1880's and 1890's, the Russian Czars mercilessly oppressed Jews with the bloodthirsty policy of the Czar's chief adviser, a fiend named Pobyedonostzev. He created a sure cure-all to the Czar's Jewish problem: convert one-third of them, exile one-third of them, butcher one-third of them.

Under such circumstances the longing for a Jewish homeland grew. The call issued by Theodor Herzl in 1896 was enthusiastically hearkened to, but it found little support from Reform Jews in America, largely because America was not Eastern Europe. We had freedom here; there Jews knew only oppression and pogroms. It was hard for Jews in America to realize that other Jews were not free to live where they wanted, earn a livelihood the way they wanted, or vote the ticket they wanted. Here, Jews sought to live and be good citizens. There, Jews found it hard even to live.

Such was the situation after World War I, even after the issuance of Britain's Balfour Declaration on November 2, 1917, which pledged His Majesty's Government to "view with favor" the establishment of a homeland in Palestine for the Jewish people. Even after Palestine became a British mandate under the League of Nations in the twenties, Reform Jewish leaders, with only a few conspicuous exceptions, did little to further the Zionist cause.

With the thirties, however, and the desperate needs created by the Nazis, Jews everywhere—in all lands, of all points of view, from all religious backgrounds—rallied together to rescue and redeem our stricken brethren. The movement to establish a Jewish state gained momentum as each DP fled Europe. By the time World War II ended, Reform Jewish leaders and laymen alike had overwhelmingly rallied to the support of the establishment of the State of Israel—a complete reversal of position since the anti-Zionism of the Pittsburgh Platform back in 1885. Yet this is only one more example of how Reform Judaism moves with the times and constantly adapts itself to the spiritual needs of our people.

Dispelling False Fears

The problem Reform Jews in America had to wrestle with over the establishment of a state was something of a philosophic problem, though no less real. What shall be the relationship of American Jews to the new Jewish state? What does this state mean to those who are American Reform Jews, American citizens of the Jewish faith, who have given their blood and treasure, their brain and their brawn, to building and defending a greater America? What should be our relationship to this state of Israel?

Very little clear thought has been distilled on the question, though plenty of emotional froth has been served up. Until 1948, the problem was *purely academic*. There were Jews who feared the creation of a Jewish state—and *fear* was the real reason behind most of the opposition to the Jewish state—fear that if a Jewish national home were once established, vicious anti-Semites would say to American Jews: "Go back to Palestine! You've got a country now! Go back there and stay there!" They feared this would become the excuse for mass expulsions, not only from America but from other countries who loved their Jews even less.

History teaches us that anti-Semitic governments have never waited for such an excuse to expel Jews. Through all the long and dreadful centuries up to the days of Hitler, Jews were driven from one country to another—not because there was a Jewish state to go back to and not because there was a Jewish national homeland internationally guaranteed. Zionism never produced anti-Semitism. Quite the contrary! Anti-Semitism created the conditions out of which arose the dire necessity of modern Zionism.

Then, too, while the problem of a Jewish state was academic, there were some Jews in America who felt that they would be charged with *dual allegiance* if they supported the establishment of a Jewish commonwealth. Here again, the enemies of the Jewish people have not waited for the creation of a Jewish state before charging the Jews with disloyalty or lack of patriotism. As long ago as the days of Esther and Mordecai, the Bible tells us how Haman whispered into the ears of the King:

> There is a certain people scattered abroad and dispersed among the peoples in all the provinces of thy kingdom; and their laws are diverse from those of every people; neither keep they the king's laws; therefore it profiteth not the king to tolerate them. If it please the king, let it be written that they be destroyed . . .[1]

Only a few years ago, the very opposite situation even produced anti-Semitic propaganda: the absence of a Jewish national center, the fact of Jewish national homelessness, became a powerful argument for the anti-Semites. The presses spewed forth from Dearborn and the radio blared from Royal Oak that the Jew has no roots anywhere, that he is an internationalist, that he has a secret international organization, "The Elders of Zion," to which he owes allegiance, that "the international Jew" is conspiring to overthrow the governments of the world so that he can seize power and rule the world!

It is impossible to keep up with the lies and calumnies of the anti-Semites. That they are contradictory, illogical, and without factual basis is of no importance. Repetition lends credence. The *Goebbels Diaries* illustrate that. If you repeat a lie often enough, people will believe it.

This much should certainly be said: the loyalties of a right-thinking American do not conflict when he supports a just cause on foreign soil. Justice Louis D. Brandeis pointed that out clearly years ago! The desire of the Irish in America to help in the establishment of a Free Ireland, or the desire of the Czechs or Poles or Greeks to help establish a Free Czechoslovakia or a Free Poland or a Free Greece do not in any way impair their loyalty to America. No one would ever accuse them of dual allegiance. No one ever doubted the loyalty of patriotic Americans who labored to pack "Bundles for Britain" or send "Aid to Russia" during World War II. In fact, when they supported movements for justice and freedom in other countries, they were

[1] Esther 3:8–9.

better Americans for having done so; they were better Americans when they tried to spread the American idea of human freedom, political equality and democratic justice.

Every President of the United States, from Woodrow Wilson on, has endorsed the idea of a Jewish State in Palestine. The Congress approved it. Our American Government has officially recognized it. Writers, editors, authors, ministers, leaders of all shades, branches and faiths, have supported the movement, and not a single one has ever raised the bogey of dual allegiance.

No, the truth is that the loyalties of American Jews do not collide but *coalesce:* they unite by growth into one body. That is the way it has always been and always will be. The establishment of the State of Israel does not alter that one iota. Jews in the United States have no other allegiance than to the United States. We are not in *galut,* in exile, here in America. *This is home for us.* We are safe here as long as democracy is safe; and if Jews, God forbid, ever find it dangerous to live in America, then democracy is doomed. The intense love of Jews for America is virtually a part of Judaism in this country. The ideals of this republic were chiseled out of Biblical granite. Mortar from the Hebrew scriptures, as Lecky observes, holds together the very foundation stones. Americanism and Judaism are so inextricably intertwined that their coalescence is complete. A former Vice-President of the United States, Henry A. Wallace, once wrote: "The Jewish tradition, the Christian tradition, the democratic tradition and the American tradition are all one."

This much of our problem then is crystal clear to all American Jews: our loyalties to America and to the American dream and our loyalties to Judaism and the Jewish people, never collide. They always coalesce and support the same ideals of justice, equality and humanitarianism.

Five Practical Relationships

In the light of all this, what is the practical relationship between American Jews and the Yishuv, the Jewish citizens of Israel?

1. The first relationship is one of *family pride.* We in America take pride in their courage and in their heroism. We reach out across the ocean and grasp their hand in comradeship to let them know that they are not alone; our prayers, our hopes, are all with them. We take pride in the new respect that the world has gained for their physical strength, for their bravery and devotion to a just cause, for the frontiersman-spirit that has transformed a sorrowful wilderness into a land flowing with milk and honey.

We and our children who stand in need of self-assurance as Jews; we whom enemies have maligned with epithets of "*Luftmenschen,* middlemen, parasites, white-collared softies, martyrs, world conspirators, sharpsters living on our wits, incapable of self-defense, self-government or self-discipline"; we who for so long have been corroded by these rusty poisons of self-hate, have seen demonstrated by the stout hearts of Israel that these are pure lies. Christian respect and Christian sympathy have been aroused. A new respect for Jewish valor, Jewish courage, Jewish bravery, Jewish heroism, have been created in the eyes of the world. We are proud of what has been done in the land of Israel against such overwhelming odds.

2. There will likewise be a *cultural, aesthetic relationship* between the Jewish communities of Israel and America. A cultural renaissance has been going on in the

land of Israel for twenty-five years and more. Already new music, new songs, new dances, new art, new literature, have enriched our total cultural heritage. We in America have already been enriched by what the Hebrew University has produced in the field of Jewish scholarship. The Hebrew Union College-Jewish Institute of Religion has opened the doors of its Jerusalem campus, where students preparing for the rabbinate will get part of their advanced training in archaeological research in Israel. A movement is now on foot to establish Reform temples in Israel. We in America have already felt the revival of interest in the Hebrew language from an ancient dead tongue to a living, spoken language as modern as the telephone and television. Statistics that I recently compiled show that among Reform Jewish congregations, the number of children who have been sufficiently interested to study Hebrew has almost doubled in the past twenty-five years. The motivation for this remarkable growth of interest is unquestionably the result of the living miracle going on in Israel. Cultural enrichment, therefore, is the second positive relationship between the American Jews and the Land of Israel.

3. A third positive relationship is *financial.* For the moment, the wheel of fate has made us the "rich relative" in the family, and the fabulous sums we have sent there thus far through the United Jewish Appeal must continue. Our Israeli brethren need hospitals, medicines, and nurses there; schools and teachers; engineers and equipment. They need the material for defense. They need the wherewithal to withstand the coming crucial years.

Indeed, we in America must give at a sacrifice today so that others of our brethren may live for tomorrow. The next few years will be crucial in Israel, and we in America, through the United Jewish Appeal, through the Bonds for

Israel program, will be called on to subscribe staggering sums. But it will not be charity. Instead, our giving will be an investment in Israel's future.

In much the same way that America was aided by foreign capital and investments during colonial times and even well into the nineteenth century, Israel today awaits development by American investors. Manufacture, industry, utilities, farming, transportation, communication, textiles, raw foods, canning, precious stones, shipbuilding, foreign trade, money and banking—a thousand different avenues of agriculture, industry and commerce await development. All these are available to American investors, both large and small. Every dollar sent to Israel is a share in her future, bringing dividends sooner than anyone can imagine. If the miracles of production achieved in the past twenty-five years are any index to what will come in the next twenty-five years, we will live to see in our time the most amazing display of human engineering and adaptability the world has ever experienced.

4. Fourthly, there is a relationship in *social service.* Here we borrow an idea from our Christian neighbors. In something like the way in which our Christian neighbors send missionaries, their choice spirits, to distant corners, in order to give personal service for a great humanitarian cause, the Land of Israel will become the missionary field for American Jewry. Some of our young men—scientists, chemists, engineers, technicians, archaeologists, doctors, teachers—will go to Israel to contribute their skills to the upbuilding of the country and then return home enriched by the experience of being part of a noble experiment. Our social dimensions will be immeasurably enlarged by these acts of in-service training, a Jewish Point IV Program of technical assistance.

5. We Americans, as loyal citizens of this great Re-

public, and mindful of our responsibilities to participate actively in the affairs of democratic government, have an obligation with respect to *American foreign affairs and national security*. It is our right, nay it is our duty, to call attention to the President of the United States, the Secretary of State, the Congress, that American strategic self-interest is involved in the Middle East; that in the present East-West conflict, we dare not permit Russia to gain a foothold there by distributing excess arms from its puppet Czechoslovakian government to Egypt and thus upset the military balance of power in the region. *Not as Jews but as Americans* we must constantly remind our elected leaders in government that it is to American interest that Israel remain secure as America's one reliable, responsible ally in the Middle East. America has had its disillusioning experiences in World War II with the empty promises, the treacherous double-dealings of Arab leaders who make a gesture of military extravagance, but whose power rests not on any popular basis, only on soil and sand—quicksand, to be specific.

We Americans must see to it that our government, along with the other great powers, guarantees the security and territorial integrity of all the countries in the Middle East, including Israel. As American citizens we should constantly articulate the need for the American government to bring about direct negotiations between Israel and the Arab states for settling their differences around the conference table instead of on the battlefield.

We Jews, as American citizens, should record our views favoring the continuance of economic and technical assistance to Israel and the Arab people as well, to raise living standards, to facilitate the resettlement and indemnification of refugees, and strengthen the democratic institutions of those nations which will promote friendship between American democracy and the peoples of the Middle East.

No Peace for Israel, No Peace for the World

The peace of the world and the peace of the Jew are one. In a mystic combination of moral alchemy, each needs the other. Neither can be complete without the other. *There is no peace for Israel, without peace for the world. There is no peace for the world without peace for Israel.* Time is running short. Because there is no peace for Israel there can be no peace for the world, and until there is peace for Israel, violence, bloodshed, hangings, machine-gunnings and bombings will continue to gut the United Nation's structure for the world. Unless frontier violence ceases and a system of peaceful diplomatic relations develops, the eager Russian bear will be only too happy to pounce upon the area and swallow up one more tasty morsel. Or to change the metaphor, if a volcano starts erupting a little lava, the lava soon spreads faster and faster, and before long covers the whole island. Our world is an island, and it may be too late for the world to realize that more than a few Israelis are at stake. Mankind is involved. The peace of the whole world is involved.

God grant that the time be not distant when in peace and accord, Egypt and Israel, and all the neighboring states, can join together not as enemies but as allies in building the millennial structure of a just and enduring peace . . . a time when "nations shall not lift up sword against nation, neither shall they learn war any more," but where every man, be he Arab or Jew, shall be able to "sit under his vine and under his fig tree and none shall make him afraid."

PART IV

INTEGRATING THE JEW IN AMERICAN DEMOCRACY

16. *WHAT IT MEANS TO BE AN AMERICAN JEW*

THERE ARE a few voices of fear in America crying loudly that being an American and being a Jew is somehow contradictory. They are saying that each of us must make a choice: shall we be loyal Americans or shall we be loyal Jews? We cannot be both, they say, because in some mysterious fashion (never clearly delineated) that involves a double loyalty, a double allegiance. I reject these voices of pessimism and fear. I maintain that being a better American makes one a better Jew, and being a better Jew makes one a better American.

It would be well for us to understand clearly the unity of purpose which forms our common denominator as American Jews. If we can have a clear concept of what it means to be an American Jew, we shall know where we are going together and how we can together face the future.

The Meaning of America

First, what does it mean to be an American? That is the first part of the problem. It means, I believe, knowing and appreciating the meaning of America.

America is more than a land, a continent full of people and prairies and resources. America is an idea . . . an idea of freedom, equality of opportunity, and fundamental human rights vouchsafed to all who pledge their allegiance to its flag. It is an experiment in social living . . . to see whether people from diverse races and creeds, from distant parts of the world, from all walks of life, can find enough good will and cooperation to make this idea a practical plan for living together.

There have been dark times in American history when we have wondered . . . when victims of hysteria and bigotry have been crucified by mob action and violent intolerance . . . when, for example, the Know Nothings of a century ago seemed to triumph with their doctrine of political discrimination . . . when the American Protective Association, the APA, seemed to forge ahead with its program of bigotry and prejudice . . . when the Ku Klux Klan seemed to win the day with its adventure in arson and terror . . . when the Father Coughlins and the Winrods and the Gerald L. K. Smiths seemed to be victorious over the Jews for purposes of political exploitation and personal aggrandizement. But always the triumph proved only momentary, because the American idea cannot be traduced by such sinister betrayals of its spirit. Sooner or later, a measure of freedom must be meted out to all Americans—or else America ceases to be America.

Lillian Smith recently wrote a moving novel called *Killers of the Dream.* Exploiters of human misery who do not understand the language of the human heart, who would turn Negro against white and white against Negro, Christian against Jew and Jew against Christian, know that democracy can be destroyed if the dream of America is killed. They are the killers of the dream—the dream of a decent society in which men will not be exploited by other men, but equity and equality will be the right of all citizens and all men can be brothers. Killers of the dream are the enemies of all of us.

To be an American means to be an American citizen —first class, not second class—enjoying liberties as of right, not on sufferance. The Constitution of 1789 made that sure. The Bill of Rights grants to every American the right to be himself, the right to be different if he so chooses, as long as he does not violate the peaceful enjoyment of the rights of others. To be an American does not necessarily mean to be the same as one's neighbor. That is Soviet Russia today. That was Nazi Germany yesterday . . . where the stamp of conformity dictated by the Commissar or Fuehrer blots out any semblance of individuality. Democracy upholds that the individual has personal rights and civil liberties with which to express his personality. *Democracy offers unity without uniformity.*

The whole history of America affirms this promise. People came to America to be different . . . to be free from discrimination, free to worship and speak and write and assemble on behalf of their own point of view. Americans have a right to differ . . . even a right to be different!

Students of democratic tradition know that these fundamental truths, on which the Declaration of Independence and the Bill of Rights are based, were distilled from the ancient Hebrew spirit: equality of all before God, social justice, and personal dignity before one's fellow-man, love of one's neighbor, understanding (not intolerance) of his point of view, inviolability of human personality. These were Jewish ethics, the very foundation of Judaeo-Christian civilization. The Jewish spirit is part of the democratic impulse of history. It preached democracy and contributed organically toward its development. American Jews have every right to be proud of the inner, organic connection between the best of democracy and the best of Judaism. There is something about a Jew that hates a storm trooper of any kind or in any uniform; there is something about a storm trooper that hates a Jew, be he bearded or shaven.

Some Americans make the mistake of thinking that all groups who have come to these shores must divest themselves of former traditions, cultures, heritages or customs in order to boil down into one indistinguishable stew . . . the old kitchen concept of the "melting pot" theory. America is rather a vast tapestry of striking colors. The characteristics of each group represent another contribution to the variety and richness of American diversity. America does not ask for complete assimilation or loss of personal identity. The melting pot is no longer the ideal. Every man has the right, indeed the duty, to be himself, as Tennyson suggests:

> Self-knowledge, self-reverence, self-control
> These three alone lead life to sovereign power.

Working for the Welfare of All

To be an American Jew means to work for the welfare of all men in our democracy. Jews are not the only ones discriminated against by an imperfect democracy. Negroes, Nisei, Catholics, Mexicans, minorities of all shades suffer alike from a problem that is basically the same.

People who are anti-Jewish find it easy to transfer their hostilities and become anti-Catholic or anti-Negro or anti-American. There is a story of a small town in California, highly prejudiced against the Japanese Nisei during World War II, where this sign was exhibited: "We are 100 per cent American—We hate Japs." The competitor across the street, not to be outdone, put up a sign: "We are 200 per cent American—we hate Japs and Jews." A third merchant, seeing the ironic humor of such phony patriots, put up a sign in his window: "We are 300 per cent American: We hate everyone!"

Freedom is indivisible. Freedom must be for all or for none. There can be no compromise.

American Jews have a particular obligation to enlist in the ranks of democracy and work for a better community. The security of Jews is assured only when the security of democratic society is guaranteed. If one man's liberties are jeopardized by communists, all men live in fear, including Jews. Jews can flourish and prosper only when all citizens flourish and prosper. Jews are safe in their rights as citizens only when all men's civil rights are safe. Jews are free to worship in safety only when religious freedom is secure for all faiths, only when church and state are separate, only when equality before the law applies to all groups, all churches, all synagogues.

To be sure, the achievement of a just society and an improved democracy is the obligation of all American citizens. Yet it devolves upon the Jews with especial directness. For we Jews have a heritage going back to the prophets and sages who centuries ago first cried out against the inequities of society. The thundering Hebrew prophets saw a vision of the Kingdom of God, not in some far-off heaven but here on earth.

Not Jitteriness But Self-Respect

So we Jews of America have an obligation to contribute our best to our homeland! We can't give less than our best and be true to our heritage!

Being an American Jew therefore requires that one be an affirmative, not a marginal Jew; positive, not hesitant. It means to be identified with his religious institution, the synagogue or the temple of his choice, searching for the faith we all need so greatly; participating actively, not just as a grandstand spectator; secure in his faith; at ease in his position; and joining hands with other men of good will in translating the principles of the three great religions into the democratic way of life.

It means to have confidence in the future of American Jewry. Some Jews feel that life in the Diaspora is futile. They consign themselves to a fate of despair, hopelessly waiting for some new upsurge of anti-Semitism to carry them off into an annihilation worse than that which befell six million of our brethren in Europe. Such is the counsel either of sincere but misguided nationalists trying to promote propaganda, or else the frustrations and penalties of being a Jew without any of the compensating joys of belonging to the Jewish people.

What a tragedy that so many Jews see only the debit side of the ledger, and feel only the liabilities without any of the assets! How lamentable that so many Jews are hagridden by this phobia of anti-Semitism and fret only because of its social stigma: they are not invited to certain parties, or can't play golf at certain restricted country clubs, or cannot live in certain suburban residential districts!

What kind of a person would *want* to sail under false colors? Only a spineless, two-faced, cringing, fawning self-seeker! For him I have less than contempt—only pity—pity that he has no pride, no loyalty, no self-respect, no peace of mind as an upstanding American Jew. Such groveling Jews are jittery because they are ignorant of the proud story of the Jewish past. They understand few of the searing lessons of modern history. Have they so soon forgotten that assimilation and good manners did not save the hides of German Jews from the Nazi soap factories or the extermination centers?

Alas, that jittery Jews are ashamed of being Jews! They are full of guilt feelings lest they be conspicuous in public life. They choose to associate only with other Jews who don't associate with Jews! They are ashamed to belong to a temple. They foolishly imagine Judaism to be full of exotic orientalisms, out of step with the occidental way of life . . . as if temples and synagogues were something to be ashamed of and somehow not in keeping with the American design for living! How little they understand the truly sincere Christian who appreciates the man of self-respect! Spiritually, such Jews (in name only) are bankrupt! Socially, they are "inbetweeners"—belonging neither to the Christian nor the Jewish community.

Oh, how badly we need well-balanced, well-adjusted Jews . . . who are at home in America, happy with their Jewishness . . . who can find from their spiritual heritage fulfillment and enrichment, fortitude and inspiration for these trying times! What a mission the rabbis of America have! What an opportunity and a challenge the temples of America have—to help make Jews appreciate their own worth and recapture their lost faith!

One of the young married women at a religious service I recently conducted, said to me following the sermon,

"Dr. Hertz, you made me feel that it is good to be a Jew." Note she didn't say "proud." Much pride is hollow and chauvinistic. To feel good about being a Jew, to be happy with one's lot and hopeful about one's future means that Judaism is teaching the rising generation a noble mission —self-respect and self-reverence.

Relating American Jewry to Israel

There is another aspect of this problem which has caused great confusion. Thoughtful Jews have perceived since the end of the Hitlerian era that with the uprooting of Jewish life in Europe and the fortunate establishment of the State of Israel, there remain in all the world only two poles of healthy Jewish life—America and Israel. By the beginning of the second decade of Israel's independence, a unique relationship has already grown up linking the two Jewish communities into a common kinship. But already there is much confusion about that relationship. After all, two thousand years of status-quo were reversed . . . two thousand years of accustomed traditions and *modus vivendi*. Some Jews immediately became phrenetic over it, full of fears and hostilities that proved utterly groundless and needless.

To be a Jew in America requires that one should be sensible about the new relationship created by the establishment of the State of Israel. Those of us who try to be sensible about our situation in America repudiate the suggestion that we are in exile. The future of American Jewry, of our children and our children's children, is linked with the fate and destiny of America. We have no alternative. We want no alternative.

The American Jewish Committee recently undertook an interesting piece of research. It took a cross-section of Jews living in New York City in fairly modest circumstances. Here is what the study learned. These Jews being surveyed regard America as home for themselves and their children. They felt a great warmth for Israel. Israel made them proud of Jewish heroism and devotion. They felt a duty to contribute financially so that Israel could discharge its heavy burdens of rescuing the many persecuted Jews throughout the world and giving them a home in which to live and labor and find security. They thought it would be nice to visit Israel on a vacation tour, but they had no intention of settling there. They felt that conditions in America are very much better and that prospects for American democracy are excellent. They maintained that the American Government alone speaks for American Jews, never the Israeli Government. They felt a kinship for Jews throughout the world based on common tradition, common religion, common problems, but kinship is far different from political loyalty. The political loyalty of American Jews is solely to the United States of America.

From this interesting study of attitudes, we can gain some insight into what the average American Jew is thinking with regard to the State of Israel. It will take time—a long time, perhaps all of our generation—for the details of this new relationship slowly to evolve. Patience, understanding, kindness and brotherliness will help much more than flag-waving or fear-mongering. One must be sensible and moderate . . . even when the finger of history is writing!

The Hour for Greatness

From all this, you can see that being an American Jew involves a sense of *noblesse oblige.* He is obligated by the noble privilege and good fortune he enjoys to stand beside those in need and extend the hand of help. Sheer luck prevailed that it was our grandfather who made the boat and someone else's grandfather, not ours, who missed it. That is about as much as we had to do with the fortunate act of being born here instead of in Germany or Poland or Russia.

American Jewry has been quick to recognize a noble responsibility to those who have not been so lucky. American Jewry has risen magnificently and written a new chapter in the book of *tzedakah*—a religious virtue in Judaism. When you look at what American generosity has done in Europe and in Israel, you begin to understand the ancient phrase of Scripture: "Charity can save one from death." And, says the Talmud, he who saves one person from death is counted as if he had saved all mankind.

But that is only half our task as American Jews. The other half, and equally important, is "to make of American Jewry the greatest Jewish community the world has ever known. That is our mandate. I'm not thinking in terms of numbers when I speak of greatness. I am speaking of greatness in terms of the spirit, of an America whose Jews read and study, who have a knowledge of their ancestral history, who are stirred with a sense of *noblesse oblige.* Never was there such a chosen generation as this, a Jewry as generous as this, as devoted, as self-respecting, as loyal and as honorable. If our people can only be enthralled with the glory of being a Jew, then we shall be able to build a Jewish life here on this soil that will produce philosophers, poets and great human beings whose achievements will dwarf the writings and the very men in whom Poland, Spain, Babylon, Egypt and Palestine once gloried. This is our hour for greatness." So spoke Dr. Jacob R. Marcus in his presidential message before the Central Conference of American Rabbis in 1950.

Truly, this is our hour for greatness.

When we understand what it means to be an American Jew, we realize that first and foremost we must be an American citizen—which means doing our part to make democracy a workable technique for individual freedom and national security.

Being an American Jew means realizing that as Jews we owe it to our country to be self-respecting rather than jittery or fearful, so that self-knowledge, self-reverence and self-control can build a solid sense of dignity.

It means a clearer, more sensible understanding of the two-way passage now being slowly developed between American and Israeli Jewry.

It means cultivating a sense of mission to make of American Jewry a dynamic community—generous, creative, self-sustaining, culturally productive, spiritually great . . . worthy of the long line of historic Jewish communities which have enabled our people to survive to this present day.

Difficult? When was it ever easy to be a Jew? Sacrifices involved? When did our forefathers ever fail to make sacrifices for their faith? Never forget that a religion which does nothing, which costs nothing, which suffers nothing, which offers nothing, which stands for nothing, is worth nothing! It is not enough merely to live! Every American Jew must live for a purpose. He must live as if he alone were responsible for the fate and future of our people.

The late Claude G. Montefiore of England once observed that ten bad Jews, indifferent and irresponsible, can help to damn us to spiritual annihilation. Ten good Jews, alert and affirmative, responsible to their convictions, dedicated in their faith, can help to save us and keep our children walking with firm step along the Jewish way of life. Which *minyan* will you join?

17. *THE AMERICAN JEW COMES OF AGE*

One hundred years ago, America was in the throes of an irrepressible conflict. Then, as now, the central problem of American democracy was color. Then, as now, the Supreme Court of the United States had handed down a controversial decision. Then it was the Dred Scott decision holding that a Negro was not a citizen of the United States and thus not entitled to all the rights and privileges of an American. Now, in our day, the Supreme Court has held that Negroes are citizens and entitled to the same educational opportunities instead of being segregated into separate but never equal schools.

One day a tall, scrawny prairie lawyer whose political reputation was still confined to the Middle West, arose before the Republican state convention at Springfield that had nominated him for the United States Senate and said, "A house divided against itself cannot stand." The Dred Scott decision of 1857 was challenged in a series of memorable public debates in Illinois between Lincoln and Douglas. Feeling rose to fever pitch as the nation was torn asunder by blood and bullets. But time and patience healed the national wounds. America grew, boomed, grew into a giant and ultimately through two world wars became a world leader. America came of age.

The American Jew, too, has come of age.

The American Jew has come a long way. He has a sense of rootage in the soil of the American community. He is part of America. He grew with America. The Jew speaks not as a stranger but as a spiritual son of this blessed land. Here he has built his home. Here he has reared his children. Here he has established his communities, his synagogues and temples, his hospitals and welfare institutions, his seminaries and schoolhouses and centers of culture. For his people, as for so many other minority groups, America has been a Promised Land "flowing with milk and honey," good to all who have contributed toward its strength.

Two Sides of One Coin

Yes, America has been good to the Jews. What was good for America was good for the Jews. Not since Hellenistic times when Jews lived in Alexandria in the second century, not since the Golden Age of Spain before the Inquisition, have Jews been so free. Vouchsafed to Jews and to all other religious denominations in America is freedom to worship, liberty of convictions, and equality before the law. Here, too, is strict separation of church and state, a blessing of freedom which few other countries, not even magnificent Israel, have been successful in achieving. Yes, America "straightened the back of the Jew," as Rabbi Abraham J. Feldman once put it. It gave him sanctuary from the indignities of European oppression that kept him from walking with head erect. No government's official church, no special disabilities, no guild's restrictive membership, no disenfranchisement of citizenship, qualified his rights or diminished his privileges as an individual. Success in the professions and in the business world depended by and large upon his ability, not his ancestry.

Yes, America has been good to the Jew, but America is also the better for it. We Jews have received much from the largess of this land, but we have also given. The reverse side of the coin applies here: What was good for the Jews was good for America! We Jews have made many significant contributions to the scientific, professional, artistic, cultural, material, and spiritual life of the land. Take almost any field of endeavor and you will find Jews whose names have become synonymous with brilliant achievement. We pioneered as humble peddlers in remote hamlets and homesteads. Brain and brawn went into the contribution of our people to the building of a new nation. We have received much from America, but we have not been empty beggars.

But this, of course, is not a new story to us Jews. It is so much a part of our being that to mention it is almost to "carry coals to Newcastle." Yet sometimes we need to emphasize the commonplace and repeat the well-known. Fresh emphasis that "Hebraic mortar cemented the foundations of this Republic" makes us better Jews when we appreciate all that our people have contributed to the making of free America.

We are Americans all. We Jews came to this continent not for gold but for God, less in search of material rewards than of spiritual opportunity—the freedom to worship the God of our fathers in accordance with our own traditions.

The freedom of the Jew to be himself was not always so, even in America. Our religious freedom was won here only by forthright and courageous determination to be accepted as equals both in responsibilities as well as privileges.

All the way back to the first twenty-three who landed in New Amsterdam aboard the St. Charles as penniless refugees from Recife, Brazil, our people had to earn the right to build their own synagogues and bury their own dead. Asher Levy, one of the first twenty-three, had to wage a bitter battle with Governor Peter Stuyvesant before he was granted the precious right of standing guard against hostile Indians. Ever since then, in war or in peace, we Jews have been proud to give "our lives, our fortunes and our sacred honor" to the defense of our country.

In the long run, however, what helped Jews helped other minorities. This land became what is so aptly imprinted on every coin of money, *"E pluribus unum"*—out of many, one! Catholics, Quakers, Jews, Irish, Negroes, Mexicans, Nisei—all learned that freedom is indivisible. It is for one and for all, or it is for none.

Happily, anti-Semitism and discrimination are not today what they were a decade or two ago. We are living in the freest time of nondiscrimination our people have ever known. True, the millennium in equal rights has not been reached. There are still peddlers of hate who want to exploit national issues like communism or the UN. They attract other hangers-on; they latch on to quasi-respectable groups. There are still troublemakers who seek to feed upon the Jews for their own petty, selfish, narrow, bigoted purposes.

We need to redouble our efforts to keep America "the land of the free and the home of the brave." This becomes a time to hold America true to the rights and liberties guaranteed to all citizens in the Bill of Rights; to renew our sense of undivided loyalty to this our only country, the last best hope on earth; to look to the government of the people to fulfil its pledges of liberty and equality for all the people without special privilege, influence, corruption or venality.

In order to preserve and protect freedom in our day and in our children's day, there are responsibilities that American Jews owe. While this country has offered opportunities for freedom, it is still riddled with unfreedoms. It becomes the solemn obligation of Jews to rally in the attack against the poor, the forlorn and defenseless; to speak up against discrimination and exploitation, against inequality or intolerance, against communism or fascism, whether imported or native born, against those demagogues who would make use of freedom to destroy rather than maintain it.

Tragically enough, we Jews have for so long been bombarded with the black nightmare of pogroms, persecutions, displaced persons, annihilation of fiendish anti-Semitism, that it is good for the soul—our souls—to be reminded of the glorious chapters in the book of American Jewish history and to recall our heroes and leaders, our men of vision and our women of valor.

Where Does the American Jew Stand Today?

It requires but a cursory glance at the American Jewish community to recognize that during the past century, and especially the last twenty-five years, the American Jew has come of age. A far-reaching transformation has occurred without our even being conscious of it. We are now overwhelmingly native-born and, on the whole, well-acclimated to American life. We have economic resources that have made American Jewry the richest Jewish community in the history of the world. Indeed, during the past decade the Jew has come upon a period of reawakening. The impact of Hitler's war upon the Jews brought many back to the fold. The crisis of war and the East-West conflict brought many, Jew and Christian alike, to realize the necessity of spiritual foundations.

Where does the American Jew stand today as he comes of age?

The Jew stands for peace, and against war. The whole Jewish tradition cries out against the hell of war, the waste of human life, the suffering and uselessness of war as a means of settling international differences. For this sputnik age, the time has come when man must learn to wage peace as hard as he wages war. American Jews wrote a glorious chapter in patriotism during World War II. Now we must learn that peace has its patriotism no less renowned than war.

The Jew stands for democracy, and against communism. The godlessness of communism, forty fiendish years in power, placing economic man at the summit of creation, runs counter to 3,000 years of Jewish theology, teaching that man was created in the image of God. In Judaism, the individual is sacred; human dignity above all else—so taught the Bible, the Talmud, the Midrash, and myriads of rabbinic teachers both named and unnamed.

The Jew stands for civil rights and against abridgments of liberty. What made America attractive to so many different strands of racial stocks, religious denominations and cultural groups who poured into these shores during the last century from every quarter of the globe was America's promise of opportunity to be oneself. Diversity and heterogeneity are our strength against the strait-jacket thought-control of a tyrannical majority. We are a nation of minorities. Therefore to safeguard the individual rights of all minorities becomes paramount. When anyone appears to threaten the security of a man's civil rights, to try them by the ordeal of slander, to traduce and villify innocent persons, be it Gerald L. K. Smith, Huey F. Long or Senator McCarthy, when a dragnet of fear is spread like a prairie fire and scars the framework of our security, then the Jew—along with other concerned fellow-citizens of all faiths—must recognize the perils to freedom and work harder than ever to safeguard civil rights. As Edmund Burke said back in 1777: "Liberty is a good to be improved, and not an evil to be lessened."

What has all this to do with the American Jew's coming of age? The Jew is first and above all else a free American citizen, like everyone else. The security of his future depends upon the future security of democracy, upon a proper balance between protecting the public good from subversives and guarding the precious liberties of individuals. He can be of help to America in her hour of destiny only if he is true to all that is best within him, true to his faith and true to his people.

And Tomorrow?

Where, then, must the Jew stand tomorrow? Where, at this great time to be alive, when America faces her hour of destiny, shall the free American citizen of Jewish faith, take his stand?

1. The Jew must preeminently be a model of the free American citizen—aware of his rights but equally aware of his responsibilities, and dedicated to the furthering and safeguarding of the rights and liberties of all.

2. The Jew must be aware of the many meritorious

and worthwhile causes that depend upon the generosity of his means for sustenance. We Jews have always taken care of our own. We have a proud and noble tradition of *tzedakah.* Whether it be the United Jewish Appeal or any one of a hundred others, we the chosen sons of Israel, blessed with roofs and warmed with clothing and nourished with food—we in America, *noblesse oblige,* cannot let down our brethren wherever or whenever they stand in need.

3. The Jew must recognize, yes, and appreciate, the noble example in democratic living which the State of Israel is giving to the world. Despite austerities in living, despite restrictions and shortages and staggering immigration, despite hostile neighbors who threaten invasion and war at any moment, Israel—mighty little Israel—is democracy's strongest outpost in the Middle East, an ally trusted and tried in the battle against fascism and communism. Whatever the Jew can do to help—be it financial aid, moral encouragement or sympathetic understanding, let the American Jew do it! Our brethren in Israel need all the help of any kind that they can get.

4. The Jew must recognize that the battle for the mass mind of America against prejudice and bigotry is far from won. Irrepressible hate groups, bordering on the fringe of insanity, are still at large, seeking to latch on to whatever groups in political life they can find. These are the troublemakers who will not rest until the Jew, the Negro, the Catholic and all the other minorities are stripped of their civil rights and scalled in public fury. To secure the rights of all people, the Jew must never give up the battle for civil rights and personal liberty. Too much can be lost for too many by puny minds who want to settle for too little!

5. Finally but foremost, the Jew stands in danger of

forfeiting through default his most precious possession—his faith. Unless the spiritual foundations are secure, human life is shaky. Man has at last learned that basic lesson. The time for a spiritual revival of worship, study and fellowship has come. It is for his mission to mankind that we have survived as Jews. Unless we stand in the forefront of such a spiritual crusade, unless we join hands and hearts with our fellow Jews in all the synagogues and temples of the land, our survival as Jews is a mockery.

We must make sure that the American Jew, who has now come of age, will prove a credit to America and a blessing to mankind.

18. *CHRISTIANITY AND JUDAISM IN AMERICA*

Recently a group of scholars gathered at Harvard Divinity School to pay tribute to Professor Harry A. Wolfson, for many years a leading luminary in Jewish studies. After a number of speakers had praised the contributions of Professor Wolfson, the guest of honor made some comments. "It is the glory of Harvard," Professor Wolfson said, "that since the time of President Elliot, the University has preserved freedom of thought, especially for unpopular ideas, and that the results of scholarly and dispassionate objectivity should be construed as evidence of the need not to destroy the boundaries but to remove the obstacles that separate faith from faith."

Areas of Agreement

The task of the goodwill movement is not to "destroy boundaries" but to "remove the obstacles that separate faith from faith." Unfortunately, much has been written and spoken about the boundaries and the obstacles, and comparatively little about the agreements between the two faiths which have been taken for granted or discounted.

Yet just think of the many areas where Christianity and Judaism agree:

They agree upon the concept of the Fatherhood of God and the Brotherhood of man.

They agree upon the rich heritage of the Old Testament and the truths and inspiration of Divine Scripture.

They agree upon the sanctity of the Ten Commandments and the Moral Law.

They agree upon the ethics of the Golden Rule, be it of Hillel or Jesus, of not doing to others what you would not want done unto you.

They agree upon the prophetic emphasis on justice, truth, mercy, righteousness, and the need to translate these ideals into the life of our time.

They agree upon the belief in the individual, in the sacredness of human life, in the inviolability of human personality, in the right of the individual to be himself and to think for himself.

They agree upon their hatred of war and their pursuit of peace.

They agree upon the democratic ideal of government.

They agree upon the need for worship and the necessity of religious education to accomplish that goal.

They agree upon the philosophic notion that life is something more than "a brilliant interlude between two nothings."

This Judaeo-Christian heritage has been a creative partnership of a common inheritance for two millennia. These decisive areas of agreement have become assimilated into the democratic processes so that today democracy is very much of an offspring of the Judaeo-Christian heritage. These are the areas of agreement where Judaism and Christianity meet. The pity is that so much more emphasis is placed upon where they part than where they meet that we too often tend to overlook those important areas of agreement!

There is an old rabbinic legend which tells that the evil judges of the cities of Sodom and Gomorrah instructed the inhabitants to set up beds on their commons. When a stranger arrived three men seized him by his head, three by his feet, and forced him upon one of the beds. If he was too short to fit into it exactly, his six attendants pulled and wrenched his limbs, stretching him until he conformed to the size of the bed. If he was too long for it, they would either cut off his legs or try to jam him in with all their combined strength until the victim was on the verge of death. His outcries were met with the words, "Thus will be done to any man who comes into our Land."

There are some who believe that it is necessary to place both Judaism and Christianity upon this bed of conformity, and by sustained pressure iron out all differences that may exist between them. Motivated by good-will, they sometimes twist and distort the essential teachings of each in order to make them identical.

Thus, "the Judaeo-Christian tradition" does not mean that Judaism and Christianity are the same, that they teach the same ideas or are therefore interchangeable. It does not mean that for the Christian or the Jew, one religion is as good as another. It does not suggest, any more than the Brotherhood idea does, that all religions are basically the same, so what's the sense of getting excited over the differences?

Recently a group of children from the religious school of a Congregationalist church visited a temple to hear the rabbi explain some of the practices and beliefs of Judaism. After the exposition a little child about ten years old said, "Rabbi, when you were telling us about the ideals of the prophets, that was Christianity you were talking about—not Judaism."

Another child hastened to add, "Maybe they're both Jewish and Christian."

In the discussion which then ensued it became evident that Judaism and Christianity shared the same ethical objectives. When the rabbi referred to "Love thy neighbor as thyself," the concept of the Fatherhood of God and the Brotherhood of Man, the prophetic quest for truth, justice, righteousness, mercy and peace, the hope of a just society that would reveal the kingdom of God on earth, the Jewish children who were the hosts claimed these as Jewish ideals. The Christian children who were the guests claimed these as Christian ideals—and they were both right!

Rabbi Ferdinand M. Isserman asked in his celebrated sermon, "The Things We Have in Common":

> What matters it to God whether men seek Him before the Ark of the synagogue, before the crucifix of the church, under the dome of the mosque, before the image of Buddha? What matters it to God whether man pray to Him in the classic accents of Hebrew, in the musical cadences of Latin, in the rhythmic poetry of the Upanishads, in German, in French, in English? What matters it to God whether men call Him Yahveh or Christ, Buddha or Confucius, Jupiter or Osiris? What matters it to God what the form of worship, what the style of ritual, what the garb of the clergy, what the theological definition as long as men seek Him with whole hearts? Then He will answer them. Therefore, even in this seemingly divided field of religion, there is unity, the unity of eternal human aspiration, the unity of worship before the Creator of the Universe.

Areas of Disagreement

There are very few Christian or Jewish scholars who suggest that a better understanding can exist between Christianity and Judaism by the sacrifice of the beliefs and teachings that are peculiar and precious to them. There *are* fundamental differences between Judaism and Christianity, which each should frankly recognize, and it is in the interest of sincerity for Jews and Christians to advocate *unity*, the harmonious cooperation of the two faiths, rather than a false and dangerous *uniformity* which would mean the liquidation of either Judaism or Christianity.[1] What then are the areas of disagreement that need better understanding by both Christian and Jew?

The most fundamental difference between Judaism and Christianity is that Judaism maintains the belief in the One God, personal and universal, whose ways are beyond understanding and whose reality gives purpose to man and to the world. No one can serve as an intermediary between God and man in the Jewish view. The Jewish tenet of the unity of God also precludes the belief in any other creative force besides Him. There is no Satan, no power of evil completely independent of God such as the devil who plays such a very important role in Christianity. In Judaism, men cannot be elevated to the stature of saints or man-gods. Even Moses is referred to as "the man Moses" so as to point out his mortality and prevent his deification.

Christianity, on the other hand, according to the Roman Catholic tradition, maintains that God is the Supreme Being, infinitely perfect, who made all things and keeps them in existence, but that God has three divine persons, the Father, the Son, and the Holy Ghost, revealed through Jesus Christ, the son of God, who teaches through the Catholic Church.

The Protestant view of God is that God is One but is manifested as Father, Son and Holy Spirit. Protestants believe in a much more individual and direct approach to God than the Roman Catholics, who believe that God can only be approached through the mediation of the Priest

[1] Rabbi William B. Silverman, Town Hall Discussions on *Judaism and Christianity Compare Notes*, mimeographed, p. 23 and following.

and the Church. In the Christian view, more stress is placed on the love of God than on the justice of God.

Miracles are unimportant in Jewish belief but rank prominently in Christianity. Judaism has consistently disparaged miracles as props of faith.

Both Christianity and Judaism have a doctrine centering around a Messiah, and a Messianic millennium of the Kingdom of God on earth. The two religions part, however, when Christianity says that Jesus was the Messiah. Judaism accepts Jesus as a child of God in the sense that all men are the children of the One Living God, that Jesus was a Jew and an inspired teacher, but with no supernatural powers. Jews do not accept the divinity or the atonement of Jesus as the Christ. Roman Catholics maintain that Jesus is the Messiah and Christ is his God-made man, that he was born of the Virgin Mary as the incarnation of God, that he atoned for mortal sin and was physically and bodily resurrected from the cross. Christ was both man and God; salvation is brought to the individual Christian through the sacrifice of Jesus on the cross, manifested in the Mass. Protestants accept Jesus as the Messiah, the Christ, the Divine son of God, and believe in a direct personal relationship rather than one through the church or through any intermediary. They believe that Jesus is a moral leader as well as the Messiah and Savior of Mankind.

Obviously, the place of Jesus is the decisive difference between Judaism and Christianity. Judaism maintains that Jesus was a Jew, not a Christian. He was born, reared, lived and died a Jew, and had no intention whatever of founding a new religion. Christianity, on the other hand, believes that Jesus was the Christ, the Messiah, announced by the Prophets of Israel and the only begotten Son of God sent on earth to bring salvation to mankind.

The religion of Jesus *was* Judaism. This we Jews do

not reject. The religion *about* Jesus became Christianity. This we Jews cannot accept.

Once Judaism and Christianity were one. The founding of a new religion was left to Paul, who constructed a theological system, far more pagan than Jewish in type, according to which man was corrupt through the sin of the first couple; and the death of Jesus on the cross was to be the atoning sacrifice offered by God Himself who gave His own son as a ransom for the sins of humanity. This doctrine he used as a lever with which at one bold stroke he was to unhinge the Mosaic Law and make the infant church a world religion. The one essential for salvation, according to Paul, was to accept the mystery concerning the birth and death of Christ after the manner of the heathen mystery religions, and to employ sacramental symbols of the mystery, the rites of baptism and communion with Christ. All this was the work of Paul.

The first disciples of Jesus, as is well-known, were Jews. The first Christian community of believers were Jews. They were within the fold of Judaism, observed Jewish ceremonies, and held strongly to the Torah and Jewish law. They differed from other Jews only in that these Jewish Christians believed that Jesus was the Messiah and had come, and that the end of the world was at hand. Paul, on the other hand, separated these Jewish Christians forever from Judaism. He extended Christianity beyond the teachings of Jesus and founded a religion separate from and independent of Judaism. He maintained that Jesus was the Christ, that the actual resurrection from the cross was central to belief and that the historical activity of Jesus as teacher of Jewish ethics should be minimized. Instead, he emphasized Jesus as the Savior, the divine son of God, who dies on the cross in atonement for man's sin.

Jewish Christians could not follow Paul in this. They

demanded that converted heathens be circumcised and accept the entire Mosaic law. Paul dispensed with both. He preached that salvation is only through Christ, which is more important than ethics. With Paulinian theology crystallized in the doctrine of original sin and the complete abandonment of Jewish law on the part of pagan Christians, Christianity became a distinct and separate religious system. It was no longer a group in Judaism, but a separate and distinct church. Jewish Christians diminished, and the pagan or Gentile Christians took over. By the first half of of the second century, Christianity and Judaism were completely parted. Christians went on as the Christian Church, but Jews went their way as the Jewish people. Each developed its own historic festivals and holidays and each gave its own people a sense of rootage and belongingness, a historic consciousness that should and can endow each individual, be he Christian or Jew, with courage and dignity.

Where They Meet and Part

Judaism and Christianity meet on the idea that both accept the Old Testament as sacred literature and assert its essential indispensability for their religion. They part, however, where Christianity adds the idea that the Old Testament is "fulfilled" by the New Testament and that the prophecies of the Old Testament foretell the events that culminate in the coming of Jesus. Jews accept only the Old Testament, but not the Apocrypha or the New Testament. The First Five Books of Moses, called the Torah, are considered basic to the Jewish faith, even though there is a wide range of interpretation by Jews of their authority, depending upon whether the viewpoint is orthodox or Reform Judaism.

Christians, on the other hand, accept both the Old and New Testament as Divinely inspired. Protestants do not accept the Apocrypha and reserve the individual right of interpretation of Scriptures. Roman Catholics accept the Old and New Testament as the literal inspired word of God, but insist that Scriptures must be interpreted properly only by the Church. They include the Apocrypha in their Scriptures. Roman Catholics do not encourage individual interpretation of the Bible, believing that the average layman does not have sufficient background, and therefore needs the tradition of the priest and the Church to interpret the Scriptures. It goes without saying that while Jews accept only the Old Testament and Christians accept both the Old Testament and the New Testament, Christians emphasize the New Testament.

Both Judaism and Christianity emphasize ethical and moral codes about pursuing the good life. Both are deeply influenced by the Old Testament prophets, preaching justice, love, mercy, truth as essential virtues to the good life. They part when Christianity insists that *not deed but creed* brings salvation. Judaism has no official creed, binding upon the individual Jew. Not his profession of faith, but his deeds must attest to his religious conviction. When Jews speak of deed, not creed, it does not necessarily mean that Jews do not have religious convictions, beliefs or philosophy. Jews have a long history and literature on the development of a body of principles.

Christianity, however, emphasizes the role of dogma. A Christian has to "believe" to be saved. Principles of conduct are less decisive to the Christian than his profession of creed, whereas Judaism emphasizes that how you live is more important than what you believe.

As for the problem of salvation, Christianity holds that the entire human family fell from grace because of Adam and Eve's original sin, but sins after baptism must be removed only through penance and absolution of the priest. Sins are carefully catalogued along with their appropriate penalties. Protestant theology maintains that original sin through Adam usually is accepted in the plan of salvation through Christ's death on the cross. Protestantism insists that forgiveness comes not from any priest, but only from Christ.

Jews, on the other hand, believe in two kinds of sins: sins against man and sins against God. On the Day of Atonement, we Jews seek forgiveness for our sins against man by seeking out those against whom we have sinned. Sins against God can be expiated only by a return to God and a return to our fellow-man. Thus, while repentance is the omnipotent cure of sin in Jewish theology, the Christian doctrine of original sin suggests the conclusion that man is too weak to repent effectively, so needs the help of Jesus. In other words, the Christian finds atonement in the belief that Jesus died for the sins of mankind.

Judaism believes that everyone must atone for his own sin, that man needs no intermediary to intercede for him. God is the Father, and a father is always near when his children call upon him in truth. While Judaism avows that God is near to every man, nearer in fact than any nearness we can imagine, Christianity teaches that God is eternally distant, removed from man who can enter a correlation with Him solely and exclusively through the mediation of Jesus, the son of God. Christianity is committed to Jesus' teaching, "Nor does anyone know the father except the son, and to whom the son deigns to reveal him." [1] This is contrary to Jewish belief which asserts that all human be-

[1] Matthew 11:27.

ings can attain to the knowledge of God through their own efforts and not as a fiat of arbitrary grace.

Thus, on the problem of ethical freedom, Judaism teaches that man is endowed with freedom of the will, solely responsible for his own decisions. Christian belief rests upon the doctrine of original sin. It posits that all men are tainted with sin because of Adam's guilt, and hence doomed. They can find salvation in the faith that Jesus died to atone for man's original sin. Since the flesh of Adam and Eve was the cause of their original sin, Christianity concludes that the body must be condemned as evil and carnal.

It follows quite naturally, therefore, that Christianity stressed the avoidance of carnal deeds and emphasized monasticism, asceticism and celibacy, while Judaism avoided such movements because it possessed not an other-worldly but a this-worldly emphasis upon ethical living.

Each Unto His Own

What does this all mean—that one point of view is right, the other wrong? That one religion has a monopoly on virtue or truth? That one religion must be accepted by all other people? On the contrary, by appreciating the vast area of agreement between Christianity and Judaism and by understanding the distinctive differences of each, what each believes about God, the Messiah, the Bible, the good life, the individual Jew or Christian should be a little more understanding, a little better person. After all, the two great faiths have a common basis and a common goal. There is no need for either to try and conquer or absorb the other. In spite of obvious differences, they have much more in common. Each should cease to eye the other like a jealous rival, and recognize instead that both are allies in the dark night's struggle to make man "little lower than the angels."

In 1779, the Great German dramatist Lessing published *Nathan the Wise,* regarded by some as the foremost plea on the stage for tolerance. Lessing was a friend of the Jewish philosopher, Moses Mendelssohn, and it is said that he patterned the character of Nathan the Jew after Mendelssohn. The scene of the play is laid in Jerusalem at the time of the Crusades. The character of Nathan the Jew, who has come to look upon all religion as forms of one great truth, is made particularly clear when a Christian lay-brother woos his adopted daughter, Recha. The theme of the play is that only by rendering justice to the Jew could a Christian do justice to himself. Finally, in a touching scene, the lay-brother says, "Nathan, sure you are a Christian, by Heaven you are, none better ever breathed." And Nathan answered, "Alack! Alack! That which makes me a Christian in your eyes, makes you a Jew in mine."

The matter is finally brought to the notice of the Sultan Saladin. Nathan's philosophy is aptly illustrated by his story of the three rings. Saladin, a Moslem ruler during the Crusades, needs funds; he tries to trick Nathan into speaking disrespectfully of the state religion, Islam. He summons Nathan and asks, "Which is the best religion, my Mohammedanism, your Judaism, or the Crusaders' Christianity?" Nathan replies with the story of the three rings which undercuts all religions that claim to possess the only "true God."

Once, says Nathan, an Oriental prince had a beautiful ring. He said he would give it to his kindest, gentlest, noblest son, who would succeed him on the throne. This bequest continued through many generations until one prince had three sons, all of equal worth. In a secret hour he had promised each son the ring. Some time later he became ill. Not wishing to break his promise, the prince had a skilled jeweler make two rings exactly like the original. Then he secretly gave one to each son. Soon after, he died. Then the three sons began to quarrel. Who had the original? In the meantime the jeweler died too. Revolution broke out. Conspiracies were formed. Bitterness was keen, until the question was referred for arbitration. The court of justice ruled: "The ring was to be in the possession of the kindest, noblest and gentlest one. None has shown these qualities in the angry quarrel. The judgment shall be deferred. Go among men, all three of you, and in time we shall determine by how nobly you have lived which of you has the genuine ring."

Then said Nathan to Saladin: "Three religions are like three rings. All have great teachings. Jews, Christians and Mohammedans alike, as they demonstrate love for humanity, sense of justice, prove theirs is the truest and best religion."

Through the play, Lessing hoped to spread his ideal of religious appreciation. When men of religion can appreciate the faith of their neighbor, when they recognize that other traditions besides their own offer rich spiritual experiences, and have encouraged sacrificial living for a noble way of life, then they have shown that they themselves possess a faith that is unsurpassed. Then the concept of "live and let live" becomes "live and help live."

RELIGION

A thousand cults, a thousand creeds,
Is one a rose and the rest all weeds;
Or is each one suited to meet some needs?
Is your own so great that the rest seem small?
Then keep it and live it, that's all.

Pagan or Christian, Gentile or Jew—
How may you know that your own is true?
Not for him or for me or for others, but you?
To live by to die by, to stand or to fall—
Why, keep it and live it, that's all.

When the strong are cruel and the weak oppressed
Does it help you to help? Does it sting in your breast?
Does it sob in your soul with a wild unrest,
To fight against might and let nothing appall—
Then keep it and live it, that's all.

—Edmund Vance Cooke

Together—or Else!

No, the battle for brotherhood is not won in the world today, even half a generation after we went to war to save freedom. Not even in America is the ideal of brotherhood secure—not as long as Jews are considered second-class citizens and denied the rights of freedom . . . not as long as Negroes are disenfranchised and segregated . . . not as long as equal rights and equal privileges to schools, housing, transportation or recreation are denied the children of the living God. Democracy is not complete until it means freedom for all—not just for some, not just for the rich, not just for white Protestants only!

Not until we translate the principles of freedom and brotherhood into the daily life of our nation will we begin to approximate what we have given our lips to: "One nation under God, indivisible with liberty and justice for all."

Differences of creed and doctrine there remain between Judaism and Christianity, and properly so; but an honest respect for differences should not mar the civic and social relations of neighbors. In matters of religious belief and practice, Christians and Jews may be as distinct and different as the fingers of an outstretched hand, but in all that makes for the economic, social, communal, cultural and moral betterment of a nation, they should be as united as the fingers of a clenched fist!

The good-will movement making alive and real the Judaeo-Christian tradition is still terribly urgent. It is still ominously relevant for our time. We Jews cannot rest on our oars or hide our heads in sand, or retreat into a narrow parochialism of our own and concern ourselves only with our own troubles. We are still involved in mankind. The plight of Israel today is a classic illustration that it is not up to Jews alone to resolve our people's problems. Mankind is involved. The peace of the world is at stake. Jews and Christians together—and not alone in America—must work together to build the foundations of a lasting peace on the basis of brotherhood. For it's together—or else!

BIBLIOGRAPHY

Some suggestions for further reading, study and discussion:

Baeck, Leo, *The Essence of Judaism,* Schocken, New York, 1948.

Bamberger, Bernard, *The Story of Judaism,* Union of American Hebrew Congregations, New York, 1957.

Baron, Salo W., *A Social and Religious History of the Jews,* Jewish Publication Society, Philadelphia, 1952.

Cohon, Beryl D., *Judaism in Theory and Practice,* Bloch Publishing Company, New York, 1948.

Cohon, Samuel S., *What We Jews Believe,* Union of American Hebrew Congregations, New York, 1931.

Egelson, Louis I., *Reform Judaism—A Movement of the People,* Union of American Hebrew Congregations, New York, 1949.

Elbogen, Ismar, *A Century of Jewish Life,* Jewish Publication Society, Philadelphia, 1944.

Fineberg, S. Andhil, *Punishment without Crime,* Doubleday & Co., New York, 1949.

Freehof, Solomon B., *What is Reform Judaism?* Union of American Hebrew Congregations, New York.

Freehof, Solomon B., *Reform Jewish Practice, Vols. I and II,* Hebrew Union College Press, Cincinnati, 1944 and 1952.

Gamoran, Emanuel, *Changing Conceptions in Jewish Education,* Macmillan Company, New York, 1924.

Gittlesohn, Roland B., *Little Lower Than the Angels,* Union of American Hebrew Congregations, New York, 1951.

Glazer, Nathan, *American Judaism,* University of Chicago Press, 1957.

Goodman, Abram Vossen, *American Overture: Jewish Rights in Colonial Times,* Jewish Publication Society of America, Philadelphia, 1947.

Gordis, Robert, *Judaism for the Modern Age,* Farrar, Straus and Cudahy, New York, 1955.

Gordon, Albert I., *Jews in Suburbia,* Beacon Press, Boston, 1959.

Handlin, Oscar, *The Uprooted,* Little Brown & Co., Boston, 1952.

Handlin, Oscar, *Adventure in Freedom,* McGraw-Hill, New York, 1954.

Heller, Bernard, *The Odyssey of a Faith,* Harper and Brothers, New York, 1942.

Herberg, Will, *Judaism and Modern Man,* Jewish Publication Society, Philadelphia, 1951.

Herberg, Will, *Protestant, Catholic, Jew,* Doubleday & Co., New York, 1955.

Hertz, Richard C., *Education of the Jewish Child,* Union of American Hebrew Congregations, New York, 1952.

Hertz, Richard C., *Prescription for Heartache,* Pageant Press, New York, 1958.

Heschel, Abraham, *Man Is Not Alone,* Jewish Publication Society, Philadelphia, 1951.

Heschel, Abraham, *Man's Quest for God,* Charles Scribner's Sons, New York, 1954.

Heschel, Abraham, *God In Search of Man,* Jewish Publication Society, Philadelphia, 1956.

Janowsky, Oscar I., *The American Jew: A Composite Portrait,* Harpers, New York, 1942.

Joseph, Morris, *Judaism As Creed And Life,* Macmillan Co., New York, 1919.

Kaplan, Mordecai M., *Judaism As A Civilization,* New York, 1934.

Kaplan, Mordecai M., *Judaism In Transition,* Behrman, New York, 1941.

Kohler, Kaufmann, *Jewish Theology,* Macmillan Co., New York, 1928.

Kohler, Kaufmann, *Studies, Addresses and Personal Papers,* Bloch Publishing Co., New York, 1931.

Kohler, Kaufmann, *A Living Faith,* edited by Samuel S. Cohon, Hebrew Union College Press, Cincinnati, 1948.

Learsi, Rufus, *The Jews In America, A History,* World Publishing Co., Cleveland, 1954.

Levinger, Lee J., *A History of the Jews in the United States,* Union of American Hebrew Congregations, New York, 1949.

Marcus, Jacob R., *Early American Jewry,* 2 Vols., Jewish Publication Society, Philadelphia, 1951–52.

Marcus, Jacob R., *Memoirs of American Jews,* 3 Vols., Jewish Publication Society, Philadelphia, 1955–56.

Mattuck, Israel, *Jewish Ethics,* Hutchinson's University Library, London, 1953.

Morgenstern, Julian, *As A Mighty Stream,* Jewish Publication Society, Philadelphia, 1949.

Philipson, David, *Max Lilienthal,* Bloch Publishing Co., 1913.

Philipson, David, *The Reform Movement in Judaism,* Macmillan Co., New York, 1931.

Reform Judaism, Essays by Alumni of the Hebrew Union College, Hebrew Union College Press, Cincinnati, 1949.

Ruppin, Arthur, *Jews in the Modern World,* Macmillan Co., New York, 1934.

Ruppin, Arthur, *Jewish Fate and Future,* Macmillan Co., London, 1940.

Sachar, Abram Leon, *A History of the Jews,* Alfred A. Knopf, New York, 1948.

Sklare, Marshall, *The Jews, Social Patterns of an American Group,* The Free Press, Glencoe, 1958.

Sklare, Marshall, *Conservative Judaism,* Free Press, Glencoe, 1955.

Schwartzman, Sylvan D., *Reform Judaism in the Making,* Union of American Hebrew Congregations, New York, 1955.

Schwarz, Leo W., *Great Ages and Ideas of the Jewish People,* Random House, New York, 1956.

Silver, Abba Hillel, *Where Judaism Differed,* Macmillan Co., New York, 1956.

Steinberg, Milton, *The Making of the Modern Jew,* Behrman House, New York, 1943.

Steinberg, Milton, *Anatomy of Faith,* Harcourt, Brace & Co., New York, 1960.

Vorspan, Albert and Lipman, Eugene J., *Justice and Judaism,* Union of American Hebrew Congregations, New York, 1956.

Wise, Stephen S., *Challenging Years,* Putnam's, New York, 1949.

1024
- 938 wet

96

327'

900'

R C Bramtley

[redacted]